FOREWORD BY **APOSTL**

# AND THEY WERE BOTH NAKED

Building an **Intimate** and **Transparent** Relationship

Be Stimulated! Be satisfied with the content of this book. Be fulfilled in your relationship!

Anto
20.1.23

CHARLES AGYEMANG ANTO

AND THEY WERE BOTH NAKED



ISBN
978-1-8380507-7-1

COVER/LAYOUT DESIGN
Bright Amoako-Attah

EDITING
Mrs. Rita Poku

CONTACT AUTHOR VIA
info@eldercharles.com

Published in the United Kingdom by

EQUIP
PUBLISHING
HOUSE

*To Phyllis, my Love for life. There is no great husband without a great wife. Your love always covers my weaknesses and makes other women think that I am an angel and the ultimate husband!*

*To Charles Jnr, Maame Yaa and Nana Afriyie. There is no super daddy without super kids! Your obedience and respect for me have made it so easy for me to be your proud father.*

“Bonding and sexual intimacy in every relationship are greatly enhanced by the total transparency of the couple involved.

Transparency in marriage is a critical and dire subject that needs the attention of not just one party in the couple but both, and a lack of it is likely to bring about a loss of trust between them. Not only is it just about the worrisome resultant loss of trust, but it is also evil and criminal to starve your spouse of truthful communication, honesty and absolute transparency in your relationship.”

# READERS COMMENTS

This book is written with the dexterity of a Counsellor, who guides the reader to assimilate the issues being portrayed in a systematic manner. It simplifies marriage issues with an in-depth analysis and gives the reader an opportunity for self-introspection. It opens the eye of the reader to the institution of marriage and how couples can enjoy their marriages forever till death separates them; and to the singles, it provides a perspective of how marriage should be and their roles in making their marriages enjoyable. I highly recommend this Masterpiece and I am dumbfounded as to why such a book had not been around to guide singles and couples alike.

***Elder Kobby Ephraim***
*Presiding Elder Crawley PIWC, UK*
*Director, Alpha Mortgage Services Ltd, UK*

Charles Agyemang Anto writes with wit and charm. This book is definitely from the Christian perspective and will help a lot of people. It is perfect for those already married. It is packed with practical, excellent wisdom, insights, and having been married for the last decade, I agree with the wisdom of the book. While engaged and newly-weds would thrive on the content dearly, there is so much value to married couples—fresh insights and timely reminders. The book covers communication, respect, trust, showing kindness to one another, forgiveness, sex and many other sensitive topics. If we can somehow figure out how to navigate all these topics overtime, we will have a successful relationship.

I also found the conclusion summarising the topics addressed, and the sentence at the end of each section, reminding us of the lessons learnt and making it even more practical, very helpful. I can`t wait for his next offering.

***Nana Adom***
*Lead Pastor, Grace Community Church,*
*Redhill, UK*

I HAVE read the whole script and will recommend it to all couples looking forward to starting the marital journey and to those with the desire to revive the joy in their marriages. There are amazing clues to a happy marriage. It is easy to read and simple to apply.

***Pastor Kingsley Akowuah-Addo***
*Head of Christian Family Fellowship, UK*
*Director of Genesis International Solutions Ltd. UK*

"AND THEY were both naked" is a thought provoking and relationship rescue book. A panacea to resuscitate broken Christian marriages and relationships. The myriad of factors discussed by the author will repair your marriage. It spells out relationship killers, means to diagnose them and renegotiate what is wrong. This book will help couples avoid divorce through the principles set out clearly to ensure good conduct among married couples. It will save your relationship when read with passion and in the fear and love of the Word of God. I recommend the book highly and unreservedly to anyone in a relationship with a fellow human.

***Dr. Eric Appiah-Yeboah*** *(LL. B, LLM, PhD in Law)*
*Legal Practitioner & Expert in Family Law - UK*
*Presiding Elder at Croydon Central, London Church of Pentecost - UK*

COUNSELLOR ANTO is not just a renowned counsellor but has also proven to be a great writer. A beautifully written and thought-provoking book which highlights all the facets of transparency in a godly marriage. A real gem of a book that creates a space for the reader to reflect on their individual actions in a marriage and inspires them to be the best in their marriage through transparency. This book is simply irresistible, and a must-read for all. God richly bless you Counsellor Anto for blessing our generation with this gem.

***Deaconess Hilda Blankson***
*Diabetic Specialist Nurse (DSN) - UK*
*LSA Women Secretary, and Women Leader, Crawley PIWC - UK*

CHARLES AGYEMANG Anto has masterfully crafted his ideas in an informative and provocative manner. His writing reveals timeless truths about the importance of transparency in marriage, authenticated by well-researched facts. I highly recommend this book as a must-read for every married couple.

***Mrs. Vida M. Lartey***
*Founder of African Women United Against*
*Domestic Abuse (AWUADA) & Parents Shield*

# CONTENTS

## Part Four - Sex and Romance in Marriage

# ACKNOWLEDGEMENTS

I thank Apostle Dr. Ben Debrah, who, in spite of his busy schedule, accepted to write the foreword of this book. Papa, I am eternally grateful for this honour you have done me.

I can also not thank you enough Pastor Nana Adom, Founder of Grace Community Church, Redhill, UK. Many years ago, you saw in me the gifts and ministry God had given me. You gave me your pulpit to talk about marriage at least twice every year. You encouraged me to write this book and you found me a publisher. To you and your wife Dr. Victoria Adom and all members of GCC, I am forever grateful.

I am also grateful to my current district pastor for Croydon, UK, Emmanuel Agyemang. When you saw the draft of this book, you encouraged me and ensured I did not delay in publishing it.

I also acknowledge former Croydon district pastor and wife, Rev Andrew Acquah and Mrs Rosemary Acquah for supporting my ministry.

My brother, great friend and coach, Rev George Lagudah and Mrs Mary Lagudah, I am grateful for your support.

I am also indebted to you my indefatigable and energetic presiding elder, Elder Kobby Ephraim. You are not only my presiding elder, but a brother and my go-to person. Thank you.

Elder Kingsley Akowuah Addo, you read part of the manuscript and provided great suggestions. I thank you very much.

I want to say thank you to Deaconess Hilda Blankson (London South Area Women's Secretary, Croydon District Women's Secretary and Crawley PIWC Women's Leader CoP) for your encouragement and support.

Deacon Obed and your wife Josephine Amoah, thank you for your constant support and for providing feedback on my marriage seminars. Jo had pre-ordered copies of this book for herself and her friends even before I put pen to paper to write this book.

I also want to thank RENEW marriages. A group comprising dedicated individuals who support me in organising marriage seminars.

I am also grateful to Rev. Douglas Asante, CEO of Equip Publishing House and his team who held me gently to make this dream of my first book a reality.

To you all who have had confidence to sit under my feet to tell me your pains, your highs and lows, and to hear my counsel, I am grateful for the lessons you have taught me about the many ways marriage will NOT work, and the many other ways to make marriage work better. And also to you all who have attended my marriage seminars on zoom or face-to-face, I am so grateful.

And finally to all you members of Crawley PIWC, I say thank you for nurturing and tolerating me all these years. I am forever grateful.

# FOREWORD

Marriage is one of God's greatest gifts to mankind. It is designed to reflect the mystical union between Christ and His church: "This is a great mystery" (Eph 5:32), according to Apostle Paul. When fully functional, marriage is like the Garden of Eden itself, providing the ambience for companionship, pleasure, procreation, raising of godly offspring, mutual help, mutual development, and fulfilling God's purposes.

Marriage's very divine origin, and potential blessing to the human race also makes it a key target of Satan. Every generation must therefore intentionally affirm the sanctity of marriage and family life as revealed by the holy Scriptures, else the very existence of society will be in danger.

*And They Were Both Naked*, I guess, is Charles' humble attempt to letting the reader into his heart to have a taste of what has sustained his marriage. Charles Agyemang Anto is an accomplished Biomedical Scientist and a respected marriage counsellor who really loves his wife. Their relationship is attractive and infectious. There is an authenticity about their love which is rooted in deep convictions and commitment.

The chapters of the book touch on various pillars of a successful marriage: the naked or transparent couple, communication, finance or money matters, and sex and romance. Charles combines his deep insight of Scriptures, his training in marriage and relationship counselling and psychology, his rich practical experience, and his excellent writing skills to expound each of these core principles for easy understanding. There are also reflective questions to engage the reader throughout the book.

The knowledge from *And They Were Both Naked* will refresh every existing marriage. The unmarried will find the book an invaluable resource as they prepare for a life-long union with their God-given spouse.

Being married myself for about 25 years now, and as a marriage counsellor and an apostle of the Lord Jesus Christ, I commend Charles for this publication, and highly recommend it to everyone who desires to develop a deeper and truly transparent marriage relationship with their spouse.

---

Ben Debrah (Apostle Dr.)
Stockholm, Sweden

# INTRODUCTION

*Therefore shall a man leave*
*his father and his mother,*
*and shall cleave unto his wife:*
*and they shall be one flesh.*
*And they were both naked,*
*the man and his wife,*
*and were not ashamed.*

GENESIS 2:24-25 (KJV)

A happy and romantic relationship is what most people desire. Who wouldn't want that? Life can be very stressful at times. After a hectic day, everyone would like to come home to a castle and a palace. We desire to be welcomed with a cheerful look from our king or our queen: a happy face, a genuine smile and a tender but firm embrace that wipes away all our tiredness instantaneously.

Many married couples are not asking for money, wealth or fame. They are not asking for an arm and a leg, or the impossible. Many couples are only looking for friendship, support, romance and genuine love. However, in a great and happy marriage, friendship, love and romance are possible only when the couple is committed to being naked and transparent.

Indeed, how fantastic marriage will be if people in love just go in with all their hearts: hiding nothing, keeping no secrets and never lying to each other! A relationship where both husband and wife are naked is likely to breed confidence and trust. Confidence and trust in each other enhance effective communication, friendship and romance. Couples in such relationships go all out to be fully naked with each other without feeling guilt or shame!

When I asked my audience in one of my seminars to use colours to describe how close their relationships were to transparency, they all sat quietly in a pensive mood.

Only one lonely voice said, "The colour of our transparency in my marriage is pitch black; probably, opaque."

This left everyone laughing, including myself. I asked Emma to explain what she meant.

"I know nothing about my husband and he does not bother to know anything about me. We have a thick wooden barrier between us. Honesty and transparency are foreign words in my marriage," she lamented.

A woman sitting next to Emma who was laughing initially said, "I now understand you, Sister. You are not alone."

Then I asked the attendees if Emma's lamentation resonated with their situations. Many of them nodded in the affirmative.

This left me thinking deeply about Emma's comment even after the seminar. I kept asking myself how many of such people living together as married couples had dark or wooden dividers between them.

In another workshop, I put the same question to the attendees. "What colour would describe transparency in your relationship?"

Not surprising, 60% of them said Red, 30% of them went for Black, and 5% of them said Cream.

"Red, because transparency is too dangerous to talk about in my marriage and it generates too many emotions when mentioned," Olivia said.

"Black, because it is difficult to see through our intents and thoughts towards each other," Frank said.

Susie said, "I don't think there are any couples who are 100% naked with each other. I know my husband and I are honest with each other but I will still not go for crystal clear, water transparency. I think the closest we can get to in our relationship is Cream."

Then all the attendees started clapping for her. They clapped not because they sided with her statement, but because they felt she and her husband had achieved a great feat, being able to describe the transparency between them with a colour as Cream. To them, that was quite a big push.

Love is amazing when you find the right person. However, when two persons are in love, what they do not easily get to know is what the other person is thinking, what their past is, and what their experiences are. Whether they are genuine and honest, we can barely know. And how can two walk happily together when they know nothing about each other?

If couples in love could come into the relationship with a clear heart and mind, marriage would be very easy. Human beings have opaque bodies that prevent us from seeing what is inside.

Even some men of God that we believe see and hear from God, sometimes have their marriages in an absolute mess. In the matters of love, it seems we are all blind and do not see clearly. This is why marriage is an interesting and very risky venture to undertake.

God only gave us a sneak peek of how a naked and transparent marriage looks through the marriage of the first-ever couple, Adam and Eve.

Our anchor Scripture, Genesis 2:24-25 says:

> GENESIS 2:24-25 (KJV)
> *Therefore shall a man leave his father and his mother, and shall cleave unto his wife: and they shall be one flesh. And they were both naked, the man and his wife, and were not ashamed.*

In this book, we shall explore if their love was crystal clear and what guiding principles made it so.

We shall also consider factors that influence transparency and intimacy among married couples. And then, recommend possible considerations that could help couples enjoy a transparent and intimate relationship.

## CHECKPOINT

How did you know your partner would be faithful, open and transparent with you before you married them? List the things that were clear indicators of this.

At this moment of you reading this book, what colour describes transparency in your marriage, and what is your reason for picking such a colour?

PART

# 1

# The Naked Couple

*Trying to live a transparent life is easier compared with trying to cover things up. It is way too much effort! In the end, you get found out and it leaves you wondering if it was worth the effort at all.*

CHAPTER ONE

# Building Transparency

The word 'naked' due to overuse, has somewhat become a cliché. I have come across names such as naked wine, naked cake, naked wire, naked fire, and even naked fruit juice! But the use of naked goes beyond that. In this book, we will use naked to denote the nature of a relationship between couples.

Naked in this book is used to refer to couples being bare, uncovered, and undisguised in their intents and actions.

A naked relationship, therefore, refers to the ability of a husband and wife, or a couple involved in a sexual relationship, to be open and undisguised in all matters relating to life and the marriage.

There are three ways of being naked. These are:

1. **Being partially naked**: This is when one chooses to be open and honest after considering whether it will favour them or not.

2. **Being completely naked**: This is when couples are fully transparent and honest in all matters, whether it favours an individual or not.
3. **Being completely covered**: This is when one decides to cover up and never be open to their spouse. Such spouses are fully covered and disguised!

As a married couple, you have the choice to be totally naked, partially naked or completely disguised. Whichever path you take has consequences on your relationship. This choice will determine the success or failure of your relationship.

Some people choose to be transparent in their emotions and behaviours but not in their finance. Some people are completely naked one day and completely 'un-naked' on most days. But your marriage or relationship stands to benefit if you both determine and decide to be naked in all matters and at all times.

*Sammy has three bank accounts with different banks in Lagos. There is a good amount of money in each account. His wife, Fonka loves and trusts him. Recently, he's bought her a brand-new car. What she doesn't know is that Sammy has a third bank account. This is the account he uses to remit his girlfriend who lives in Abeokuta, Nigeria. Fonka only gets to know this when his girlfriend traces Sammy to their matrimonial home to leave their (Sammy and his girlfriend's) son because she (the girlfriend) wants to marry someone else. Fonka has only been aware of two bank accounts and has never had knowledge of the third account, or that her husband Sammy is having extramarital affairs.*

*"I am completely shattered; I am broken and I do not feel I can ever trust any man. I trusted Sammy and gave all my inheritance from my late father to him. But now that he has stabbed me in the back, I am going to seek divorce and get all my dad's estates back."*

Being un-naked or partially naked can be very costly as can be witnessed from the scenario above. As long as you have not been exposed, you feel you are smart. But it takes too much effort to cover up. Usually, you have to tell a lie, and then keep telling lies to cover up your previous lies until you no longer remember your lies. You get caught in your own web. Sometimes, God decides to lift the 'veil' after He has presented you with many chances to come clean and you fail to take those chances. God will defend the poor and the defenceless. He will also defend the just and the righteous. At that stage, you fall on your own sword. Shame and disgrace become your companions.

Your marriage will struggle if only one of you is naked. For your marriage or relationship to thrive and be successful, it requires both of you to be sincere, honest and naked.

## IS SUCH A RELATIONSHIP POSSIBLE?

Yes, couples can and should be totally naked in every aspect of their lives.

When couples agree to marry, they are declaring to themselves and all witnesses that from that day forward, they have agreed to share their bodies, wealth and life together. The success of their relationship will severely be affected if one or both parties feel ashamed to be truthful and honest in any of these areas. The importance of transparency in every marriage cannot be overemphasised. It is transparency that transcends into intimacy. That is why any little kind of disconnection or misrepresentation in the marriage can cause havoc in the relationship.

## DEFINING TRANSPARENCY

The Hebrew word for 'ashamed' is 'bush' which means disconnected, or disappointed (by reason of acting shamefully).

The Cambridge Dictionary defines ashamed as "feeling embarrassed, or guilty because of actions, characteristics or associations."

The question that I get asked all the time is, "How can couples be truly transparent?" Let's give answers to this question by looking at 'transparency' from these perspectives:

- **Your Physical Bodies**

In fact, this is the beauty of marriage. Marriage provides the legal grounds to share not just your estate or money, but your body as well with the person you love. There is no marriage without the sharing of bodies. There are no limitations or hindrances to you sharing your bodies as a married couple!

You should be comfortable being naked in front of each other, feeling no sense of shame or guilt!

**1 CORINTHIANS 7:4 (NIV)**
*The wife does not have authority over her own body but yields it to her husband. In the same way, the husband does not have authority over his own body but yields it to his wife.*

It is this equal share that some refer to as 50/50 but I call it 100/100. If I marry you, you cannot travel with my body if I do not agree to it.

Your body may be round or square, big or small; it does not matter. You are just madly in love! You are just eager to undress in front of him or her. It is important that you do not pass negative or derogatory remarks about any part of the body of your spouse to make them feel ashamed. When couples appreciate their bodies, they are likely to give 100% of themselves to each other.

If you have this understanding, when your partner requests for sex, you will not deny him or her. If your spouse asks you out, you will not say you don't feel well. That also means that if you feel pain, your partner should also share in that pain because you share the same body. You are to sympathise and not ask your spouse for sex, or ask them out when you are well aware that they are not well or indisposed for good reasons. Couples who are united have both empathy and sympathy for each other. They feel each other's pain and tears.

A husband and wife should be able to indulge in all kinds of activities, including playing with each other and the kids without finding it shameful. In fact, enjoying each other's folly, jokes, flaws and still not being ashamed is the point couples must get to.

Apostle Paul suggested that a man and a woman should marry for the following reasons:

i. to avoid burning with passion
ii. to control their sexual desires
iii. to share their bodies

And this is in agreement with Genesis chapter 2:

i. leaving your family to cleave to your partner's body, soul and spirit
ii. being naked and unashamed, once married

It is also true that some men and women can be a bit selfish or domineering and will control the appetite of their spouses. They decide when they want to touch you and when to be touched.

> *Jude 41 said, "I thought I was marrying my wife Rita so that I could have sex any time I wanted. I was wrong. When I need sex, I have to bribe her with something. It could be money, doing the cooking the next day, bathing the kids or dropping her at work twenty miles away. She has total control over my body and her body. I have control over none."*

Unfortunately, that is what some couples have to deal with in their marital homes. This can be very dangerous to the health of such a marriage. Such relationships are likely to fail at some point unless the playing field is levelled.

### Your Past Life and Experiences

Each of you might have past or present experiences that you cannot share with friends or family because you are not proud of them. But when you marry, you should have no shame revealing them to your spouse. You should not be embarrassed to share such experiences with your spouse because you trust them, and you know you will not be judged harshly. If you do not want to be judged, then you should also not judge the past behaviours, actions and attitudes of your spouse, which they have repented of.

### Your Money and Wealth

> *"With all my earthly goods, I do wed thee."*

If you said this vow honestly, then you should disclose all your money and wealth to your spouse! You should not be ashamed if you earn little and you should also not be proud if you earn more. Do not hide your income from your spouse just because you earn more than they do. Transparency should be practised at all times and not only when it is convenient for you.

### Tightening Your Intimacy

Couples can build transparency and strong intimacy in their relationship by consistently engaging in these activities and more: having more sex, showering together, cooking together, chatting, joking, kissing, hugging, holding hands, praying and playing.

## CHECKPOINT

What were some of the things you considered before choosing your spouse? Was transparency one of the things?

CHAPTER TWO

# Marriage Made in the Garden of Eden

*Adam and his wife were both naked,*
*and they felt no shame.*

GENESIS 2:25 (NIV)

If your marriage was made in heaven, then you have no business disturbing people on earth. Marriage is for people on earth and not for heavenly beings. If the marriage that was made in Eden suffered attacks from the devil, then you must understand that your marriage will be no exception. Be ready to fight for your marriage.

A marriage made in the Garden of Eden! Wow! How amazing that must have been. Just the husband and his wife, with their friend God in the Garden.

The marriage made in the Garden of Eden is the one that has come closest to perfection. Adam and Eve were naked to each other. Nothing was disguised. All things were bare! They had all that they needed to enjoy their marriage and each other. They had gold on the land, a beautiful garden, and a perfect temperature and atmosphere. They went through no stress and no pressure! There was zero interference and no competition! No rent to pay, no bills and no daily commute. No sweat and hard work were required of them. They knew no hunger, anger, tears, cold, flu or infections. In fact, coronavirus would not survive there!

All that was required of them was to enjoy the beautiful garden and admire nature and God's creation. They only had to look after the garden and the giraffes, parrots, lions and birds and aquatic creatures; have sex and have children. Lastly, they had the great opportunity to enjoy a sweet and intimate relationship with themselves, and with God. This was the first love and first marriage!

If you were Adam and Eve, would you swap that for our current hassle and bustle lifestyle?

To many couples, first love is the sweetest time of their lives. No wonder the Bible admonishes us to remember our first love. Usually, the couples are green, innocent and so loving. Couples in such relationships are in competition for kindness, honesty and transparency. They have great attachment and bonding! They want to open up their chests to reveal all that they have inside. I know this because I have been there before.

When there is pure, undiluted love, marriage is heaven. I should say the relationship is heaven. It is full of kindness, patience, goodness, joy... You may add yours to this list. The aroma spreads across every environment. It is pleasant, sweet, delicious and beautiful. The couple wants to share all they have together. That includes their time, money, life and of course, their bodies.

God created Adam and Eve without coverings and placed them in the Garden of Eden to marry. It is interesting that God did not give them any covering. It was Not accidental; God did not forget to give them covering. He was deliberate about it. It was orchestrated by God Himself. Aside from it being a test of obedience, it was also to become the model or standard for future marriages.

I guess while in the Garden, they were not just naked. They were holding hands, eating and drinking and visiting friends together. I guess they went out shopping and yet were very comfortable. I guess nobody cared that they were naked, and nobody was ashamed because they were both the same.

Adam and Eve being naked meant:

1. They had nothing to hide from each other.
2. They had time to spend with each other.
3. They were content with all they had.
4. They did not have to work hard for any material needs.
5. They depended totally on God for all they needed.
6. They had clear minds about each other.

## EVEN GOD WAS NOT ASHAMED OF THEIR NAKEDNESS

If you've ever believed that being physically naked offends God, then you probably have to think again.

Understand this: even God was not ashamed of Adam and Eve's nakedness. On the contrary, God loved their nakedness, openness and transparency. Before man sinned, Adam communicated with God in his nakedness; yet, God was happy with him. I can imagine Adam and Eve worshipping and praising God without shame. God was never embarrassed by that.

They were content and happy with each other, and God. Their friend, God appreciated the naked bodies He had given them. In fact, God came in the cool of the day to have fellowship with them, in their nakedness.

> PSALM 100:3 (NLT)
> *Acknowledge that the Lord is God!*
> *He made us, and we are His.*
> *We are His people,*
> *the sheep of His pasture.*

God is more interested in having fellowship with us everywhere we are—whether at church, at your workplace, in the bedroom or even in the bathroom—than our physical nakedness. Couples should make it a priority to engage with God any day, anywhere.

## NO MARRIAGE IS IMMUNE TO ATTACKS

Life was great and fun. Marriage was amazing in the Garden. But this was not going to last long. Adam and Eve disobeyed God. They rejected His friendship and kingship. They thought life outside the Garden will be better.

They were probably bored with just the three of them in just one location. They rejected their nakedness and sought covering. Anytime man thinks he deserves more or something better than what he has, it ends in disaster. If you feel you deserve a better husband or wifc than what you have now, be careful! It may be the beginning of your marital disaster. Adam and Eve tried it and it ended badly. Your marriage has opposition and adversary. The devil is clever and persistent. Both husband and wife must work together to overcome him. If one of you loses focus, and begins to look at other things, you invite the old serpent—the snake who is still an active and powerful predator as he was in the Garden of Eden—into your marriage. See what he did to the first couple:

> GENESIS 3:1-10 (NIV)
> *1Now the serpent was more crafty than any of the wild animals the Lord God had made. He said to the woman, "Did God really say, 'You must not eat from any tree in the garden'?" 2The woman said to the serpent, "We may eat fruit from the trees in the garden, 3but God did say, 'You must not eat fruit from the tree that is in the middle of the Garden, and you must not touch it, or you will die.'" 4"You will not certainly die," the serpent said to the woman. 5"For God knows that when you eat from it your eyes will be opened, and you will be like God, knowing good and evil." 6When the woman saw that the fruit of the tree was good for food and pleasing to the eye, and also desirable for gaining wisdom, she took some and ate it. She also*

*gave some to her husband, who was with her, and*
*he ate it. 7Then the eyes of both of them were opened,*
*and they realised they were naked; so they sewed*
*fig leaves together made coverings for themselves.*
*8Then the man and his wife heard the sound of*
*the Lord God as He was walking in the garden in*
*the cool of the day, and they hid from the Lord God*
*among the trees of the Garden. 9But the Lord God*
*called to the man, "Where are you?" 10He answered,*
*"I heard you in the garden, and I was afraid because*
*I was naked; so I hid."*

**WHEN DO MARRIED COUPLES FEEL ASHAMED?**

1. When they are disconnected from God.
2. When they follow other voices instead of God's voice.
3. When they use their own strength and ability to seek wealth.
4. When they seek other friends outside their relationship.
5. When they begin to tell lies.
6. When they prefer to spend time elsewhere.
7. When they no longer see any good things in their marriage.
8. When they focus their attention on material things instead of God.

**CHECKPOINT**

List some of the things that happen in your marriage that make you really happy. Are there some things in your past or present life that you are ashamed to let your spouse know about?

## LESSONS FROM THE GARDEN OF EDEN

From Genesis 3:1-10, there are a few things we must guard against. These include:

- Opening your eyes wide after marriage. Their eyes are being opened. It is important to open both eyes before marriage and shut one after marriage!
- Listening to other voices instead of holding on to God's instructions. There is always another voice to distract your marriage, shut your ears to them.,
- Making coverings. Innovations and creativity are great. But be careful you do not pierce your marriage with any knives. Avoid shades that are false shadows!
- Hiding from the Lord in the bushes. This is the worst a man can do, rejecting the friendship and authority of God in your marriage. Even in bad times remember God is on your side.

The following lessons can be drawn from the first marriage God instituted in the Garden of Eden:

## When God Is Your Friend, You Can Lack Nothing in the Marriage

Adam and Eve had no craving for anything so long as they were obedient and kept fellowship with God. God became their provider and source of provision for all their needs. Ah! This reminds us of Jesus sending the disciples out:

> LUKE 22:35 (NIV)
> *Then Jesus asked them, "When I sent you without purse, bag or sandals, did you lack anything?" "Nothing," they answered.*

Indeed, if the Lord is your friend and provider, be assured that you are covered! Marital life in the Garden was as good as gold. It was glorious.

They had nothing to complain about because God took care of them. When God was their friend, Adam and Eve never had needs and so never complained of lack or want. They did not compare themselves to friends.

If you and your spouse will allow God to be your King and your God, then you will know that He is too strong to fail you. He has everything. And you will lack nothing because He is your shepherd.

You might think that the world has moved on and life has become more complex than in the days of Adam and Eve. Listen, they had their own challenges and limitations. The current dispensation also has its own challenges and limitations. But the principles are the same —when you and your spouse are honest with each other, life tastes sweeter. If you depend on God as your friend, He is able to supply all your needs.

Adam did not have anything of his own, and neither did Eve. They shared all that they had. No clothes or covering meant that there was no pocket to hide anything from each other. It is in every couple's interest that they are both obedient to God. It is in your own interest that your spouse takes the things of God seriously. When you support each other to grow and mature in God, you both become honest and totally reliant on God. This will do your marriage a lot of good. Marriage in the Garden of Eden was great so far as God remained their covering and friend!

**CHECKPOINT**

Adam and Eve lost God and their marriage in the Garden of Eden. What lessons can you learn from this?

## Be Careful Who You Call Friends — They May Be Enemies to Your Marriage

GENESIS 3:7-8 (NIV)

*"Then the eyes of both of them were opened, and they realised they were naked; so they sewed fig leaves together and made coverings for themselves. Then the man and his wife heard the sound of the Lord*

*God as He was walking in the Garden in the cool of the day, and they hid from the Lord God among the trees of the Garden."*

When Adam and Eve were together, they did not only enjoy themselves, but they also enjoyed their marriage and their relationship with God. Unfortunately, this joy did not last long. Eve might have been bored just living with Adam as most of us have the tendency to become, at certain points in our marital journey. She found comfort in the company of the serpent. Among all the creatures in the Garden, why did she choose the serpent? Look at what the Bible says about the snake:

GENESIS 3:1 (NIV)
*"Now the serpent was craftier than any of the wild animals the Lord God had made. He said to the woman, 'Did God really say, 'You must not eat from any tree in the garden?'"*

The snake was not only crafty, he was also a smooth-talker. He managed to steal the mind of Eve. We are not told how many times Eve hung out with the serpent. But we know that it ended badly. Not only did it affect their marriage but posterity and every generation from then.

We all have friends in our lives, but what kind of friends do you keep?

I have friends for different reasons. When I need financial advice, I know who to call. When I have medical issues, I know who to call. These friends are not just friends, they are my coaches. With certain friends, we only talk about football, and nothing else. But I have one or two mature friends I talk to about my marriage. I am a friend to my wife's friends and vice versa. You should be open about your friends outside your marriage. Whether the same or the opposite sex, your partner should have a say in who you hang out with.

Couples have a duty to protect each other from any unscrupulous or unsuspecting friendships which might hurt their relationship with each other and the marriage.

> *Getty said, "I observed this lady in church who would not invite anyone else to pray for her apart from my husband. She was not married. I sensed by her actions that she fancied my husband. When I told my husband to be careful and not to visit her alone, he was furious and did not speak to me for three days, even though he is an elder in the church. Rather, he would speak to this lady every day. Two days after we spoke about it, he took her food shopping. Two weeks later, she reported my husband to the pastor that he had raped her. My husband has been suspended from the church and the case is now in the hands of the police."*

### Don't Hide From God or Your Partner

Is it not interesting how we always gravitate towards friends and families when we have issues? You see, when you and your spouse are intimate, you want to be around them all the time. But when the relationship turns sour, what happens? You are angry and upset. You just don't want to see them. In fact, you just want to do anything to avoid them even if you have to take extra hours after work. Some people will go out with friends in the name of 'work do', 'leaving do', blah, blah, blah! Those who are bosses come home very late, ostensibly coming from a 'Board meeting'.

Check this Scripture again:

> **GENESIS 3:7-8 (NIV)**
> *"Then the eyes of both of them were opened, and they realised they were naked; so they sewed fig leaves together and made coverings for themselves. Then the man and his wife heard the sound of the Lord God as He was walking in the Garden in the cool of the day, and they hid from the Lord God among the trees of the Garden."*

Ah! You are not alone! It all began with Adam and Eve. When they offended God, they lost confidence and courage to look into His face. They made no attempt to seek forgiveness. They thought it was time for independence; that it was time to enjoy married life without God's constant visit. They forgot that their lives did not belong to them. God created them, and God had total control over their lives.

## Their Eyes Were Opened When They Were Supposed to Be Half-Shut

> *"Keep your eyes wide open before marriage and half-shut afterwards."*
>
> **BENJAMIN FRANKLIN**
> (American Writer, Scientist, Inventor, Statesman, Diplomat, Printer, Publisher and Political Philosopher)

The eyes are killing so many men and women. They fancy whatever they see. The question is, who or what have they been seeing?

> *"Then the eyes of both of them were opened, and they realised they were naked; so they sewed fig leaves together and made coverings for themselves."*

Why didn't they know this all the while? What you are realising now, what or who hid it from you before? Who bewitched you? If your friends do not have the mind of God, they may tell you many things outside the will of God. Weigh the intents and counsel of your friends. Those who make you feel you are too naked, that you are too low, and that you deserve better and so on, you have to be careful with them!

Lack of contentment can drive couples to seek pleasure and solutions outside their marriages. When you are enjoying your marriage and family, you are blind to any outside influence. But when the marriage turns sour or ugly, there is the tendency for any of you to seek external support. This help may be sought from the same sex or the opposite sex. Usually, if this support is sought from the opposite sex such as a work colleague, it can lead to flirting and extramarital affairs.

A husband and wife have a duty to protect each other's eyes by satisfying their curiosity at home. Some people have fantasies, which is normal. So, it will be great to be open and honest with each other about your fantasies. Love is great at sharing and sharing is about everything. Your husband or wife should feel free to talk and do all things with you. In fact, it is better to satisfy your curiosity and fantasies with your spouse than to practice them with someone else.

**They Sowed Fig Leaves, Creating Artificial Barriers**

Adam and Eve moved away from God's provision to self-reliance. How did they do it?

They made coverings for themselves. God was their real covering. After the disobedience, they took on fake coverings.

The Psalmist says, "On Christ the solid rock I stand, all other ground is sinking sand."

Be careful about any advice, suggestions and proposals from friends that are not godly. Improvise is not the real deal. Your partner cannot be compared to a friend or a family member. Value your relationship with your spouse and your God. Three is stability!

Fig leaves means disguising and covering things up. It means a lack of transparency, honesty and openness in the marriage. When you choose to put on fig leaves or look for any coverings, they will mask your marriage. The fig leaves in your marriage could be: financial infidelity, extramarital affairs, keeping a secret in your past life, or hiding certain behaviours or conditions. Even if you made a mistake and you slept with someone, you have a duty to be open and honest with your spouse. Covering up your errors and keeping secrets is only a temporary solution, which can have long term consequences on your relationship.

## Adam and Eve Hid Themselves in the Bushes at the Sound of Their Friend God

They probably did not realise that God is all-knowing and present everywhere. They were seeking a life away from the Source of their lives. If Adam and Eve had shown remorse, they could have been reconciled to their friend God. They would have done themselves and the world good. Couples have a choice to work to bring peace into their marriage or just break it. Hiding solves no problem. Running away from your partner instead of saying sorry is a sign of pride and arrogance. I know some people will not even say sorry to God, let alone to their husband or wife. That was the attitude of the fallen Adam and Eve. Hide no more from God, He is on your side in this marriage. And do not run away from your spouse when a little misunderstanding arises. Seek to make peace with God and with your spouse if you want to enjoy sweet fellowship and your marriage.

## Don't Leave God Out

When Adam and Eve sinned, they did not like to be naked. But that was the cause of their struggles, hard work, labour pain and sin. They did not need money to buy clothes. They did not need to farm to get more fig leaves when they were naked before God. After the fall, they had to work hard to maintain their new life. God did not suggest anything to them nor provide for them anymore. When you leave God out in your marriage, be prepared for the consequence!

Marriage tastes sweeter, creates better bonding and friendship if we are naked with each other and with God.

## Beware of Any Forbidden Tree in Your Marriage

GENESIS 3:7 (NIV)

*"When the woman saw that the fruit of the tree was good for food and pleasing to the eye, and also desirable for gaining wisdom, she took some and ate it. She also gave some to her husband, who was with her, and he ate it."*

The woman Eve dared God: "Let's eat and see what will happen," she might have said to her husband Adam. They paid a heavy price for this. Every person has something that gets under their skin. Try to avoid this to maintain peace and harmony in the home. Do not tempt your spouse with what she or he is weak at. If your spouse has a weakness in sexual fidelity, then you have to make sure that they are not starved at home. If you know a work colleague has a crush on you, don't go out with him or her. To some ladies or gentlemen, it is their money. If you misuse their money, they may not be able to forgive you. Be transparent but be wise in your relationship.

**CHECKPOINT**

Is there anything you have learnt from Adam and Eve, the first couple ever?

CHAPTER THREE

# *Secrets and Dishonesty in Marriage*

*"Do not lie to each other, since you have taken off your old self with its practices."*

COLOSSIANS 3:9 (NIV)

No amount of prayers will be effective if you are filled with lies and secrets in your marriage.

Naked couples strive to be honest and truthful because of their love for each other and Christ. When your relationship is shrouded in lies and secrecy, not only does it cast doubt about your love for each other, but also the genuineness of your faith in God. Many Christians are suffering from the damaging effect of keeping secrets in their marriage and from their family. They are constantly in the church, visiting pastors and prophets supposing that their powerful prayers will heal their mental and physical traumas. Sadly, they have never considered that they are the cause of their own disease and trauma. This chapter gives you insight into the effect of your actions and how you can be healed.

## SECRETS AND LIES HURT YOUR MARRIAGE

Lies are the beginning of a relationship breakdown. It can bring down the strongest, fortified walls of security and trust.

Lies and secrecy hurt all relationships, just give it a try and see.

> *When Elder Dankas' daughter Abigail came home in tears, he thought he knew what had happened. "Frank has laid his hand on her again," he thought.*
>
> *He was wrong. It was not that this time. Abigail had uncovered a big secret! Frank had two children in Ghana with his girlfriend. She had chanced on receipts of money transfers he had been sending to this girlfriend back home. Abigail has lived in London since age ten. She met Frank on Facebook and within 6 months, the couple got married in Accra, Ghana. Abigail worked hard to get enough money to bring Frank over to the UK a year before the incident. The couple seemed happy until Abigail began noticing that Frank hid when making phone calls. If she chanced on him whilst on a phone call, he would quickly end the call. When she complained about it, it led to a heated argument. Frank pushed her, she slipped and fell. She went to her Dad's house to complain. Elder Dankas persuaded her to be patient. After discovering that Frank already had two children and that he still remits his girlfriend, she just wanted the marriage annulled.*

Lies, cheating and keeping secrets are some of the main causes of separation and divorce among couples. When couples are neither communicating nor connecting, there is usually something fishy going on in the marriage.

Honesty and openness enhance every relationship. A marital relationship that is full of lies and secrecy can be likened to driving a car with a flat tyre and refusing to change the tyre. It is only a matter of time before an accident would occur. It is, therefore sad that many marriages these days suffer from lies, cheating and secrecy. This is one of the biggest problems in many African marriages, especially those in the Diaspora.

Don't try to be too smart, you will be found out. Don't lie and keep secrets, and yet expect your partner to be honest with you.

Once in a while, we all do not tell the whole truth. Some of the lies and secrets are quite minor and harmless. These include the number of past girlfriends or boyfriends; how clever we were in secondary school, and things like that. These do not bring much harm to our marriages.

However, certain lies are pathologically harmful to you and your marriage. These include: not telling your spouse of children you have before the marriage ceremony is held; your immigration status; your health status; your debts, and financial status. If you lie or keep secrets in any of these areas, you are putting your marriage at risk.

Researchers assert that the average person keeps at least thirteen secrets. In a survey of 2,175 married Brits, conducted by a UK family law firm, Slater & Gordon, 20 percent said they are keeping a major secret in their marriage. About one in four of those people said that the secret they're keeping is so big that they worry it would end their marriage (Taryn Hillin, 2014).

- 25% of respondents who admitted to lying admitted they had kept a major secret from their spouse for more than 25 years.
- 12% said they had gone to extreme lengths to hide it.
- 28% believed that telling the secret now would make things worse.

Keeping important secrets from your spouse is not only unfair, it is also disrespectful.

*In the case above, when Abigail attended counselling, she said: "I have given all my world to Frank, thinking I have a brother, uncle and a husband. He has my bank details and even my internet banking password. I never knew he would do such a thing. How can I trust him again?"*

*Abigail had had a difficult upbringing in London and lived with her dad alone. She had purposed that she would team up with her husband to create a family that was together and intact. Even though Frank admitted that he feared that if he informed her of the remittances to the ex-girlfriend with whom he had the two children, Abigail would be upset, Abigail said she would have been okay with it if he had discussed it with her.*

The success of a marriage is greatly enhanced by the openness and honesty of the couple. Couples, families, children and societies stand to benefit immensely if couples would be sincere, honest and trustworthy in their relationships.

**CHECKPOINT**

What is your opinion about being transparent in your marriage? Is it a price too much to pay?

## RISKS ASSOCIATED WITH SECRETS AND LIES AMONG COUPLES

### Health Risk

A secret is something done, made or conducted without the knowledge of other people. When one of those people is a spouse or partner, we wonder not only why, but also how it jeopardises that relationship.

Scientists believe that not all diseases are caused by infection or the devil. Keeping secrets, lying and cheating on your partner have health consequences.

> *"When we keep secrets or are being deceptive because we think we'll be rejected by people, it increases the body's insulin and cortisol, which can create heart palpitations and affect the brain."*
>
> DR. JOHN PAUL GARRISON
> (Clinical and Forensic Psychologist)

This can lead to:

- Irritable bowel syndrome (IBS)
- Anxiety
- Diarrhoea
- Chest pains
- Hypertension
- Cardiac diseases
- Abnormal lung function
- Diabetes

*(Virginia Pelley, 2019)*

A renowned minister of God in a popular Pentecostal church had great wealth. His wife had no idea how much the husband had. The man kept all his assets and money secret from his wife who had left all she had to follow the husband in doing the work of God. She was faithful to him but the minister was not. The minister had hypertension and diabetes which his wife was helping him manage. But he did not respect her. All the time, he would say, "When I retire, I am going to enjoy all that God has given me." A few days to his retirement, he had a brain haemorrhage and stroke. This affected his mental capacity which meant he lost his memory. He lived for a couple of years and died.

GENESIS 2:25 (NIV)
*"Adam and his wife were both naked,
and they felt no shame."*

Couples must understand this: there is a price and wage you pay for your actions, whether good or bad. Sadly for married couples, there is an even a greater price to pay for being dishonest and secretive. Apart from the price you pay when caught, there is also a heavy price you pay on your health and wellbeing.

Diseases are awful. They are not pleasant. I am a healthcare professional, and I see people struggle all the time. I see people take cups full of medicines morning, afternoon, evening and night, and yet do not get better. This must not be your portion in Jesus' name!

Of course, not all diseases are caused by our sins or errors. But as much as it depends on you, let no disease come upon you as a result of your errors and sins.

### Spiritual Death

When you cheat in your marriage, you do not just cheat your spouse; in fact, you cheat yourself because you and your spouse are one in marriage.

Some couples are dead in their homes. This spiritual death arises as a result of their lies and dishonesty. They lie to themselves, to family, and to the government for everything, including social benefits. As if that is not enough, they lie to God as though God can't see or that He is not omnipresent.

> ROMANS 3:23 (NIV)
> *"For the wages of sin is death,*
> *but the gift of God is eternal life*
> *in Christ Jesus our Lord."*

You see, when you divorce your spouse for benefits or a council house, you will live in that house alone. Don't be deceived, our God honours agreements between people!

MATTHEW 18:19 (NIV)
*"Again, truly I tell you that if two of you*
*on earth agree about anything they ask for,*
*it will be done for them by my Father in heaven.*

Your marriage was not acceptable before God because of the golden ring, the beautiful gown or the powerful prayer by the minister. It was accepted due to the agreement and the witnesses that were present with you.

Keeping lies and secrets violates the covenant and vow you took in the presence of God and all who witnessed the ceremony.

*Anna is a Zimbabwean working as a nurse in the United Kingdom with her husband Anthony who works as a security man. Anna says, "I thought getting a council house was the best thing that ever happened to me. What I did not know was the consequences of telling the council I was divorced. Just one year after getting the house, my husband left home and now lives with another woman. I thought I was helping the family but it has made all of us worse off. I am now planning to give back the house to the council. I want to be reconciled to my husband and my God.*

Spiritual death has dire consequences and must be avoided at all costs. To the couple and the family, it is like driving a car with a sleeping driver. The family is heading in only one direction—a ditch! Souls will perish. This includes your children. If you don't want to perish here on earth and in hell, then do this one thing:

**EPHESIANS 6:14 (NIV)**

*"Stand firm then, with the belt of truth buckled around your waist, with the breastplate of righteousness in place."*

**CHECKPOINT**

What are some other damages that marriages suffer from lies and dishonesty?

CHAPTER FOUR

# Couples' Authentic Behaviour and Emotion

*"It's like a video panel, you know that? Your face. I don't think you realise how much of what happens inside you that can be seen in your face. Maybe it was just me. I paid attention to you."*

JULIO ALEXI GENAO
(An American Independent Editor and Writer)

*"Having an authentic emotional response is always a positive thing."*

YAEL COHEN
(South African-Canadian businesswoman, and a Co-founder of Fuck Cancer, a health organisation working for early detection and prevention of cancer)

Everyone admires couples who have genuine chemistry between them. As a couple, your children, family and friends are watching if you are genuinely in love. Your spouse, your family and friends also want to see if your words match what you do. When you both sit on a sofa, how much of a gap is left between you? When you say I really love you, how much eye contact do you make with your spouse? And when you say I am sorry, what does your body language also say?

If you are a minister of the gospel, when you stand at the podium and you want all people to know how much you love your wife, what do you do after the sermon or service is over? Naked couples ensure that their actions match their words! Naked couples have also excelled in understanding their spouses' unspoken feelings and behaviours.

A feeling or behaviour is said to be naked if it is undisguised and uncovered. Stress, sadness, upset, joy, happiness, insecurity and excitement are some of the emotions every human being experiences with time. Great couples are those who have adapted to each other's moods, feelings, emotions and behaviours. They have also built good trust and understanding to be able to express how they feel, both in bad times and good times. Their husbands or wives have become their friends, confidants and counsellors.

Couples benefit greatly if they are open to each other in things that upset them; things that make them miserable, and things that make them happy. Many husbands are deficient in this area. So ladies, make it clear what makes you happy and what makes you sad. Do not assume your husband will pick that up straight away. Some men are amazing but do not bet on all men doing so.

It is also important to be able to tell your spouse how you're feeling and why you are feeling that way. It is a two-way channel. You also need to make yourself available and receptive to your partner's emotions.

Behaviours and habits such as shouting, kicking or slapping each other, and/or the kids, break the marriage. We all have some habits that no one has managed to tell us. They annoy some close friends and colleagues but they have not managed to tell us. If you have a naked relationship, your partner will feel free to correct you lovingly and gently. But if there is no transparency in your relationship, this can affect your relationship with the outside world and can cause you shame.

**DEAN AND AMINA**

*Dean says when they were dating, Amina was the most cheerful and pleasant person to hang out with. But three years into their marriage, Amina has changed. She is moody and unapproachable. Dean says, he does not have the guts to discuss how he feels and this is drawing them apart.*

*When they visited the counsellor, Amina revealed that Dean has many behaviours and habits that upset her. When she tries to bring them up, Dean either grows cold for over a week or shouts at her. After he has come out of his "shells", he behaves as though all is or should be normal. When Amina was pressed to name some of the habits, she said, "This includes using the toilet without lifting the toilet seat; placing his dirty clothes anywhere instead of putting them in the laundry basket, and being too loud in public."*

We form feelings, habits and behaviours over time. Couples should correct each other with love. If there is love, humility and honesty, such attitudes can be talked about informally. Couples should find it acceptable to be corrected by their spouses. Emotions should never be used to correct each other; otherwise, the correction will be ineffective.

**CHECKPOINT**

How comfortable are you, expressing your feelings or sentiments to your spouse? List the things that upset you that you want your spouse to take notice of.

CHAPTER FIVE

# Reasons Couples Fail to be Transparent

Being secretive or superstitious is not godly because in Christ the veil that divided the temple has been torn into pieces. Couples should not create any more veils in their marriages.

When your spouse decides to lie or to be dishonest or insincere with you, they may have many reasons for doing that. But there is always one fundamental reason: fear.

## FEAR

Fear makes people lie, hide and even run into more serious problems.

Let's see what happened in Genesis 3:10;

> *"He answered, 'I heard you in the garden,*
> *and I was afraid because I was naked; so I hid.'"*

Adam in other words was saying, "I cannot face You again. I have not obeyed Your commandment. I have been disobedient. I am ashamed to be Your friend. I am afraid you may scorn me, insult me, beat me or even kill me."

Fear causes a lot of havoc in the life of humankind. Fear makes people have heart attacks and consequently, die. If people can talk you into becoming afraid of something, they have you in their pockets. This is the strategy the devil uses to control people.

*Eva had multiple abortions before she met Eric. She is aware she is unable to have babies but has hidden this from Eric. To add salt to injury, the couple planned how many children they would like to have and which primary school they wanted them to attend even before the wedding ceremony.*

*After three years of failed attempts at having babies, Eric finds out that his wife Eva cannot bear him a child. Eric is seeking divorce.*

In the story of Eric and Eva above, why do you think Eva kept her infertility a secret? Do you think if she had revealed it to Eric early, it would have changed their story?

I am sure you agree that she feared the worst, letting Eric in on this one. During counselling, it came to light that Eric started talking about children right from their dating days. Eva showed signs that she was uncomfortable but feared if she disclosed it, Eric would not marry her. Eric insisted Eva should have given him the option to make his own decision.

It is true that when couples cover things up, they probably are afraid of:

- The reaction of the other person
- Being rejected
- A possible disagreement
- Confrontations
- Loss of trust
- Loss of relationships
- Loss of reputation
- Loss of income
- Loss of jobs
- Being punished

## SUSPECTING YOUR PARTNER IS NOT NAKED

When you suspect that your partner is hiding something or not being truthful, the natural tendency is that you also take cover. Couples should not give room for suspicions.

## FEELING EMBARRASSED

When there is pressure to help the family back home all the time, one person may find a way of covering up if they feel their partner will be unhappy about it. Some couples do not really want to cheat or lie in their relationship, but when they feel embarrassed by the constant demand for financial help from their family and friends back home, they tend to lie to cover up the shame of burdening their spouses with such demands. Couples must have a conducive platform to talk about everything without feeling ashamed. Make your spouse feel welcome bringing up every issue. Do not ridicule or mock them.

## LACK OF AGREEMENT

Some partners right from the onset decide to keep their monies and projects separate. They agree to let each one have the freedom to enjoy their own wages. Such an agreement may work if there is understanding. Unfortunately, it can end up creating much bigger problems if not handled properly. Who is paying what at home? In the end, one partner usually feels angry and cheated and this creates a lot of problems and insecurities.

## HAVING SECRET MOTIVES

When a partner has a secret agenda or motive in the marriage, such persons hide their payslips, bank accounts and even their projects. It appears they are not in the relationship for the long haul. It is just a matter of time. It is dangerous to play with someone's heart. It is fair to marry people you love. If you don't love them, at least, it is morally right to be fair to them. You see, God fights for the poor and those who are cheated. You might not get away so freely.

## SUPERSTITIONS

Some people read meaning into everything and that includes even seeing an ant in their rooms. They have rituals and mysteries to everything. They include things practised in the Old Testament that held the people bound.

*When Stella came for counselling, she said, "Elder, there is a room in our home I can't enter because it is a private room where only my husband goes to pray. When I am having my menstrual period, my husband does not sleep on the same bed with me. My husband does not want us to discuss any issue at night because he believes witches and powers are all ears at this time so we barely resolve anything in the marriage."*

Some people have certain clothes they wear to preach believing that they contain the anointing of God. All these are superstitions that have been born out of fear or from their family of origin.

Christians must not fear any demon or witches because those who are with us are more than those against us.

Listen to what the man of God said to the servant,

2 KINGS 6:16-17 (NKJV)
*So he answered, "Do not fear, for those who are with us are more than those who are with them." And Elisha prayed, and said, "Lord, I pray, open his eyes that he may see." Then the Lord opened the eyes of the young man, and he saw. And behold, the mountain was full of horses and chariots of fire all around Elisha."*

## CHECKPOINT

What are some of the reasons why you hide things from your spouse? How has that affected your relationship with your spouse and children?

CHAPTER SIX

# Characteristics of the Naked Couple

*"A long-lasting marriage is built by two people who believe in and live by the solemn promise they made."*

DARLENE SCHACHT
(American Evangelical Christian author and blogger)

If you have any reason not to be honest or sincere before you enter into any relationship, then your love may not be genuine.

Honesty in a marriage is so important. You can't build a strong relationship on half-truths and half-lies. Be honest at all times.

Couples who are naked have many fine characteristics: they pray together; they both invest in their marriage and have no fears. They are both cheerful, love to spend time together, their children are nice and well-behaved, and their home is warm and welcoming. They support each other to improve upon themselves, they have projects together; they hide nothing including money, and they know and approve of each other's friends. Such couples do not only spend quality time together, they also rejoice and celebrate life together.

Let's delve a bit deeper into the main characteristics of naked couples:

## NAKED COUPLES ARE BEST FRIENDS

> PROVERBS 18:24 (NIV)
> *"One who has unreliable friends soon comes to ruin, but there is a friend who sticks closer than a brother."*

I have always held the opinion that if your spouse cannot be your friend, you are already a loser. Married couples are not just sleeping partners. They are not just friends: they are intimate friends. My wife is not just my friend; she is also my confidant, my advisor, and my number one fan. She is my coach and my master. I don't just listen to her, I believe her counsel.

Couples who are naked to each other have telepathic understanding. When they are in separate places, they both tend to think about the same thing at the same time. One of my pastors used to say that when he is preaching and his wife is not in the congregation, he does not preach well. This is because he says he derives his vigour and support from his wife. You see, such couples do not just love each other, they are intimate friends, physically and spiritually. I have also seen some men of God whose wives struggle to sit in the congregation to listen to them. They are not enemies but they are not a fan of each other.

God loved His relationship with Adam. But God realised that Adam needed a person of a similar body, who is like-minded, and touchable or relatable. Someone he could have a good laugh with. And someone he could not live without. Eve was therefore created to be a companion and a good friend to Adam. Eve was not an afterthought. God wanted Adam to experience loneliness first so that he could appreciate Eve when she came. God wanted Adam to be the forerunner to Eve. So, Eve is not inferior to Adam. On the contrary, she is the real deal. I am incomplete without my wife Phyllis. When your spouse is your best friend, it increases the attachment and bonding between you. All couples should work hard to make their partners their best friends.

### How Do You Do That?

- Study to understand your spouse's personality and what has shaped them.
- Always start a conversation about what they are interested in.
- Try doing things together. Things that both of you love to do: cooking, gardening, walking, painting, etc.
- Spend time touching, hugging, kissing, relaxing and sleeping together.
- Above all, try to avoid criticising each other.

*Dan says, "I have always suspected I am probably the 3rd or 4th most important person to my wife. This has become clearer since our children left home. I feel like a stranger and a loner in my house. My wife goes to the church's women's meeting one time, then it is the Gambia society meeting the next time, or a friend's party. When she is home, she is on the phone with our children. No problem. Next, she is on the phone again with her cousins, aunties, brothers, sisters, and former boyfriends. It is crazy! This marriage is going nowhere. I need another friend and companion."*

If your spouse is not your friend, they will need another friend, especially when the children leave home. Make your spouse your friend now to save your marriage.

## NAKED COUPLES ARE EAGER TO SPEND TIME TOGETHER

*My perfect day has nothing to do with*
*the weather or what I'm doing.*
*My perfect day is whenever I'm with you.*

ANONYMOUS

One of the greatest gifts you can ever give to your loved one is quality time. Who you spend your time with shows where your heart is!

For couples to stick together, they must spend enough time together. Naked couples are eager to spend time together. Sleeping, praying, walking, visiting friends, eating and even bathing together help enhance your bonding. Naked couples are so open that they fully know their partner's itinerary. You see, the moment Adam was not in the company of his wife, Eve had another friend who misled her. Couples must understand that two heads are better than one. The enemy can deceive one person easily but when the two are together, it is more difficult to deceive them. When you are together and make decisions together, you are more likely to get it right. Spending time together does not mean you have to be in each other's pockets. Naked couples spend time together, and they also allow each other the space to grow and fulfil their God-given potential and ministry.

> *Esther 28 is married and comes from Lagos. "One of the reasons that got me into marriage was seeing a couple coming from the bathroom together," she said. "It was my prayer to have a man to spend quality time with me. Unfortunately, my husband Ed prefers to play chess with his mate. I am second to his friend."*

Couples who are naked yearn to speak to their partners. They can't wait to see them after work. They want to spend time talking about work, children, what to eat, where to visit on holiday, achievements and even their challenges.

## NAKED COUPLES PRAY TOGETHER

Such couples identify issues in the family and come together to discuss them, and pray about them.

> *Mr and Mrs Abia discovered that their teenage daughter was showing signs of pride and disobedience. One Saturday morning, they called her into their bedroom. They discussed their observation with her and thereafter, prayed with her.*

The couple then put her on their prayer list. Anytime the couple had a morning devotion, they prayed for her. Four weeks later, Emma came and confessed that some friends were leading her astray and that she had broken ties with them. They thanked her for her obedience. They gave glory to God for answered prayers.

> *In another development, Mrs Abia came home from work with a sad countenance. When Mr. Abia enquired, she revealed that she had made a serious mistake at work and that she felt she might be penalised for it. Mr Abia assured her of his support and of God's presence which is with them always. The couple organised a 2-day fasting straightaway for God's intervention. One week later, she was called by her manager for promotion for her honesty when the incident happened.*

When couples are naked, they are one in spirit and willing to support each other and the family with prayers.

## NAKED COUPLES ARE HONEST WITH THEIR FINANCES

Money is great, but the love of it has wrecked too many marriages. One way to judge if a couple is in love and open to each other is by checking their feelings towards their monies. When you love someone, you do not only give them your time but you also enrich their pockets and meet their needs.

Couples who are in love and naked do not only sleep together, they share everything, including money.

In relationships where there is no transparency, there is a yawning gulf between the couple with regards to how each manages their finances. When couples are honest, open and transparent, their monies are also disclosed to each other and managed together.

If you can hand over all your income to your spouse, damning the consequence, then your heart is truly committed to him or her.

If you can sign a blank cheque for them to request any amount required, then your relationship is a diamond. In fact, you know they have an idea about the bank balances so they would not overdraw.

If you can hand over your online banking login details to your wife or husband just in case they need money, then you have a crystal clear relationship.

It is easy to say with your lip that you love him or her. But are you committed to your words? Do you tell the whole truth or a half-truth when it comes to your finance?

Remember they were both naked. It is unfair to expect your spouse to be transparent when you know you are not.

Naked couples do not allow money to be a standing block in their marriage. Always remember that they were both naked.

Issues on financial transparency are discussed in detail in the second part of this book.

## NAKED COUPLES ALLOW FOR MISTAKES

No one goes through life as a superman who never fails. Everyone is vulnerable. Only Jesus was not.

When I tell you my fears, I am not weak and do not seek sympathy; rather, I am being open to you.

Life is full of surprises. Sometimes the most careful people are overtaken by events and fall into traps. No one is immune to temptations. Do you remember what Jesus said to the Pharisees?

> JOHN 8:7 (KJV)
>
> *"So when they continued asking Him,*
> *He lifted up Himself, and said unto them,*
> *'He that is without sin among you,*
> *let him first cast a stone at her.'"*

It is easy to be critical of your partner when they make mistakes. Naked couples accept everybody makes mistakes and learn from their mistakes. It is part of the growing process. Nobody really wants to make mistakes but it is something that happens to all mortals. Naked couples have understood this and allow it to go because someone has also forgiven them.

**CHECKPOINT**

Which of the lists above do you practise in your marriage? List also the ones you practise but were not mentioned.

CHAPTER SEVEN

# 10 Simple Ways to Bring Openness Into Your Relationship

*If it is possible, as far as it depends on you, live at peace with everyone.*

ROMANS 12:18 (NIV)

*Love is patient, love is kind. It does not envy, it does not boast, it is not proud. It does not dishonor others, it is not self-seeking, it is not easily angered, it keeps no record of wrongs.*

1 CORINTHIANS 13:4-5 (NIV)

It is important to encourage each other to learn to be transparent in the marital relationship. To do that, practise the following:

## ALLOW EACH PERSON TO LEARN FROM THEIR MISTAKES

If you accept you are both human and mistakes are part of the experiences needed to grow up or mature in certain aspects of our lives, you will be calm if one makes mistakes. People cover up mistakes and faults if they fear your criticism and reprisal.

## FORGIVE EACH OTHER QUICKLY

There is no need to hold onto someone's mistakes and keep reminding them. There is no need to be bitter and unforgiving when your partner does something wrong. Remember you also make mistakes, and your partner bears with you. Your friends, your family and colleagues bear with you when you are broken by your mistakes. Above all, Christ has and continues to forgive your sins or mistakes. Christ wants us to do the same for other people. If you forgive others their wrongs, why can't you forgive your spouse and family for their wrongdoings?

## SHOW EMPATHY FOR EACH OTHER'S WEAKNESS

There is a proverb that says, "Do not hit a man when he is down." No one takes delight in making mistakes.

> *"When I make a mistake, I am already beating myself. I do not need another whip from my husband," says Sandra.*
>
> *"It will be nice if my husband will just put his arm around me and say, 'Honey, I understand how you*

*feel. Don't worry, all will be fine.' This will take a lot of pressure off me. And I will be happy to talk to him on any other matters." says Philippa.*

**SUPPORT EACH OTHER TO GROW**

No one is a finished product. Growth is a process and not an endpoint. Do not see your spouse as having finished growing. When you marry, you are prepared to not just sleep together but to rise together, walk together and grow together. You are going to grow in character, spirituality and physicality. Marriage is a long haul. It requires your patience and support to help each other grow. Do you think you have helped your husband or wife grow since you married?

**BREAK DOWN THE WALLS OF DEFENSIVENESS**

A culture of intimidation and criticism has a negative effect on your spouse and the family. One of such effects is everyone avoiding you and hiding from your presence. They will build a defensive wall around themselves so that you do not penetrate to get to them with your words and/or actions. Couples who are naked do not build defensive walls because they do not need to. They live in an environment of freedom and openness. They have both taken time and effort to build such a relationship. It is lovely and it is enviable. If your spouse or children do not feel free to tell you anything, please sit back and reflect on your approach to correcting and criticising their mistakes.

## UNDERSTAND EACH OTHER'S BACKGROUND AND WHY YOU ACT THE WAY YOU DO

Naked couples have taken time to study the background and upbringing of their spouses. They can easily predict how they will react or respond to many issues. They understand and feel for each other. They also know and understand that it will require time to get over and transform from certain behaviours and attitudes. Therefore, they give themselves more time to get over such attitudes and behaviours.

> *Sam said, "I do not come from a privileged background as my wife. My table manners are not great. My bathroom manners are not great either. I have lived by myself since I was 15 years with no responsibility to anyone until I married my wife a year ago. It has been an eye-opener. My wife revealed all my flaws and deficiencies within one month of marriage. I now feel nervous and lack confidence. I just want to run away from her."*

You should not expect instant change from all the things you see in your spouse as faults. Remember it has taken them several years to cultivate that and you will have to give them time.

## ACCEPT YOU ARE IN THE MARRIAGE FOR LIFE

Marriage is not a sprint race: it is a marathon. The fact that you have started ahead of your spouse does not mean you are better. Your educational qualification may be higher today but a few years into your marriage, the narrative could be different. In the course of your marital life, there are going to be many twists and turns, ups and downs. You will face many difficult situations and choices that will require the assistance of your spouse or family.

> *Grace has this narration, "My husband never accepted me as equal when we got married because he was a medical doctor and in his own words I was just a primary school teacher. He will shoot down any ideas and suggestions from me. He embarrassed me privately and publicly, sometimes in front of his friends. After all, he is the doctor, breadwinner and Mr Know-it-all. Then one sunny day, he ignored my advice, as always, not to drive after a few beers. He was involved in a serious accident and got his two legs amputated. He is now at home feeling miserable. I am now in charge. Sometimes I want to pay him back in his own coin."*

If you despise your spouse now, when you need them in times of trouble, they might not have a good heart when helping you. We all need somebody; if not now, it may be later. Wise couples stick together so that when adversity comes, they will be able to stand against it.

## APPRECIATE EACH OTHER'S CONTRIBUTION

You should give room to talk about all the big and small things. If you value the contribution of your spouse, your communication will improve drastically. The reason your spouse does not want to engage or contribute to any conversation is because of your dominance. You want to dominate and win all discussions. After all, what is the point of wasting one's time if the spouse doesn't listen?

> *According to Paul, "Debbie thinks she knows everything I am going to say. So before I even open my mouth, she puts words into my mouth, and they are almost always wrong! She doesn't understand I am a man with my own mind. This is the reason I do not open up to her."*

**RESPECT EQUALITY IN EVERYTHING**

One secret of a successful marriage is treating each other fairly and equally. You see, God knew He had deposited a lot in Adam but Adam still needed help. Eve also had many abilities but needed Adam to make them complete. This is the beauty of marriage. Let's see how the Bible puts it.

> GENESIS 2:24 (NIV)
> *"That is why a man leaves*
> *his father and mother*
> *and is united to his wife,*
> *and they become one flesh."*

One flesh simply means you are inseparable. Irrespective of what you think you bring to the table, it does not make you a higher shareholder in the marriage. Your gender, status, qualification and riches should rather make the marriage better. It does not make you better than your spouse. Naked couples are not doctors, lawyers, politicians or pastors at home. They are simply a husband and a wife when home!

## COMMEND AND APPRECIATE EACH OTHER

Have you watched athletes running? Do you see how they get extra energy to run when they reach where their fans are cheering them on? Marriage is like that. You need to cheer each other on with praise and encouragement. If you praise your spouse all the time, I can tell you they will be drawn toward you all the time. Praise is a magnetic force that pulls your spouse towards you and nothing resists it. Find something nice to tell your spouse each day.

**CHECKPOINT**

Thinking through the points above, which of them do you feel you need to improve on to have a better marriage?

PART

# 2

# Couples, Communicate!

*If you are a man and you do not want to talk, find someone but a woman to marry.*

*"I think men talk to women so they can sleep with them and women sleep with men so they can talk to them."*

**Jay McInerney**
(American novelist, screenwriter, editor, and columnist)

CHAPTER ONE

# Communicating Without Fear and Boundaries

Naked couples do not only communicate; they communicate freely without fear.

Every living creature communicates. Human beings communicate. A husband and wife communicate.

The importance of communication has been emphasised over the years. Many people including pastors, counsellors and psychologists have tried to guide couples on how to communicate properly in marriage. I do not know if this has always worked.

You do not need a communication degree to marry. You don't have to be a great orator like Bill Clinton or Barack Obama to communicate in your marriage. If you are a public figure, the way you address your employees, board of directors or your nation will be different from how you address your wife and children. I doubt anyone would ever address their wife and children at home as "Ladies and gentlemen, or fellow citizens ...". You see, the language we use at the workplace, parliament, the church pulpit etc., is totally different from what we use at home. Presidents have to show seriousness, put on a straight face and deliver what has been written for them.

In marriage, you do not need a scriptwriter. You do not have to be serious all the time. Sometimes, you talk to your children and wife or husband with jokes. You maintain affection and create fun for good laughter.

The truth is that whether you are blind, deaf, or physically challenged, you still have a way of communicating with people for them to understand and appreciate your needs. Even when you are not uttering words, you may be using non-verbal cues like gesturing with your hands, feet, eyes, face or any part of your body; laughing, smiling, whistling, etc, as a means of communicating your feeling.

## WHAT MAKES GOOD COMMUNICATION?

Good communication is not only about the number and volume of Words you utter. Good communication has other components such as Tone of voice and Body Language. Psychologists believe these three form the basis of effective communication. But the fourth component which is the feedback is equally important. These components are so important in our everyday conversations at work, home or anywhere else.

Psychologists and researchers however agree that the most important of them all is Body Language, followed by Tone of Voice and then Words. They have tried to give percentile points to these three. These percentile allocations vary from researcher to researcher. But overall, body language is given 50-55%, tone of voice is 35-38% and words are given 7-15%.

Where there is communication, there must be a speaker and a listener. But communication can only be complete when there is feedback between a speaker and a listener. The feedback can be verbal or non-verbal. Effective speakers and listeners learn how to receive feedback either verbally or through body language.

## BE AN EFFECTIVE SPEAKER IN MARRIAGE

It is important to stress that, when you are speaking you do not just rattle 60 words per minute and walk away. You might not get the attention of your audience or spouse or even your children. When you speak with grace, a good tone of voice and at a measured speed, everyone just wants to listen to you. Good speakers also have good control over the volume, tone, and pitch of their voice. It is not only about what you say, it is more about how you say it. Your posture, focus and facial expression also add great value to your communication.

Depending on an individual's background and education, they may be perceived as loud and arrogant. Others can also be perceived as timid, shy and soft. Some people are classed as persons of few words whilst others are known to be professional talkatives.

Good couples give each other equal time and space to speak. They are patient with the one who is slow to speak. Those of us who usually speak for a long time, supposing that the many words we speak will change people are not always right. Good communicators do not have to speak millions of words to be heard.

Effective communication is even more important when you are talking to your spouse over a means which does not give them the opportunity to see you. At such times, your spouse will use your tone of voice, punctuation and other means to judge or discern your attitude, personality and willingness to do something. Shouting, screaming and hurrying in your voice or writing expel helpers and friends, and most importantly, your spouse. A voice that is calming, gentle and assuring breaks the wall of resistance of even the most stubborn person.

So, the next time you are talking to your spouse on phone or by mail or letter, be mindful of your tone. Let your voice or tone of writing do the job for you. Let it be soothing and refreshing.

## LEARN TO LISTEN

To be a good listener, you have to learn to give your full attention to your spouse when they are speaking to you. Do not give room to any interferences that can distract you. To do that, you ought to look into the eyes of your spouse when they are speaking so that you can connect with him or her. You have to give your undivided attention. Also, show interest in whatever conversation you are having by asking questions, paraphrasing, summarising and nodding. Apply appropriate non-verbal cues when communicating.

You can teach some of these but others have been formed from upbringing. How couples communicate will depend on the level of understanding between them. Couples who are naked feel free to talk and discuss any issue.

Naked couples are also great at reading body language to understand the feeling of their spouses. Again, they are prepared to give their full attention when they are having a casual conversation or a deep discussion. They are happy to discuss any issue at the right time and place.

You see, naked couples do not need to be experts in communication to be good at it. Communication evokes attention, feelings or emotions. Couples who are naked have adapted to each other so much that they don't make light of words uttered in good faith. They do not suppress their emotions per se but they are able to respectfully express how they feel to their spouses, and their partners also take time to listen to their concerns.

> *John says, "I knew I talked fast and loud, and sometimes used unacceptable words. But Faustina has helped me to talk better and even listen better. I am one of six children raised in a harsh environment. I do not have a higher educational qualification compared to Faustina. But she has been patient with me and I am grateful."*
>
> *Faustina also confirmed that when she met John, she just loved him for his energy, enthusiasm and hard work. "He is chatty and funny. That was all I needed from a husband. Then I realised that*

*his communication can be improved and I was prepared to help him. I knew he would let me because he is humble and keen to learn."*

## DO NOT IGNORE FEEDBACK

It is important to understand that feedback can be both positive and negative. In couples' conversations, feedback comes in many forms. These include:

- **Verbal Response**

*E.g. Husband:* "Amma, my mom wants to visit us next week if that is okay with you."

*Wife:* "Oh! That will be brilliant. I miss Mummy so much."

This is positive verbal feedback.

Alternatively:

*Wife:* "Again?"

It is one word, but it is negative feedback.

- **Facial Expression**

Same question:

*Husband:* "Amma, my mom wants to visit us next week if that is okay with you."

She frowns and says nothing. This is a response but negative feedback.

- **Body Language**

*Husband:* "Amma, my Mom wants to visit us next week if that is okay with you."

This time, Amma just turns away from her husband, and while leaving, supports her chin with one hand, and says nothing. That one too is a response but negative feedback.

- **Voice Inflexion**

Inflexion is various changes in your voice as you speak. This includes the emotions and anger in your voice that make you speak faster or louder.

> *Eg.* Amma tries to talk but her voice shakes at the utterance of Mom visiting. This is also negative feedback.

Husbands and wives who pay good attention to these will not only avoid unnecessary conflict, but will also please their spouses.

> *"When I am discussing a sensitive issue with my wife, I check for feedback all through the conversation. If I get a nodding of the head, a lit-up face or positive comments, I get the energy to continue. In case I get silence, turning away from me, or a frowned face, it tells me I should either drop the conversation or ask her to express how she feels verbally just in case I am reading her body language wrongly," said Kobby.*

*Matt was upset that Mavis did not prepare meals for the family when he returned from work. He had already had a rough day at work and was expecting to find comfort in his Friday jollof rice.*

*"You have been sitting at the same spot since I left for work. Quite disappointing that there is no food in the house," Matt lamented, almost shouting.*

*Mavis tried to speak but she broke down in tears. Matt failed to read from her facial expression that Mavis had taken ill all day. In fact, she was sleeping when Matt entered the house.*

*When Mavis composed herself, she asked, "When have I ever made you go hungry?"*

You can see from this scenario that Matt failed the body language test. Mavis spoke very little but her statement was powerful. Couples must read the body language and facial expressions of their spouses. Even if you do not want to talk, your feelings are usually expressed on your face.

**CHECKPOINT**

Apart from the few points we have discussed, is there any area in your communication you feel needs improvement?

CHAPTER TWO

# Non-Verbal Communication in Marriage

*"No man is truly married until he understands every word his wife is Not saying."*

UNKNOWN

*"Language is a more recent technology. Your body language, your eyes, your energy will come through to your audience before you even start speaking"*

PETER GUBER
(American business executive, entrepreneur, educator and author. He is Chairman and CEO of Mandalay Entertainment.)

Nonverbal cues or signals consist of body language, gestures, postures, gaze, facial expressions and the space we give to each other when upset. It is something we do every day, mostly unaware. That is why experts believe it is the most genuine and purest representation of your behaviour and thoughts. They believe that you can take all your time to plan and articulate what is in your mind, but what your body says is your truest self. Experts argue that if couples take good note of these cues in specific and general situations, they can better understand their partners' moods, emotions and level of connection between them.

This is because every part of human anatomy can speak without uttering a word. The interpretation of nonverbal language is subject to the interpreter and it can vary from culture to culture or country to country. When couples are intimate and naked, they fully understand every expression either on the face, in their eyes or through touch on any part of their partner's body.

If couples master this type of communication, it can be life-saving in difficult situations. Nonverbal communication is not only about your body language, it is also about your feelings and the inflexions in your voice. It is also the colour in your face, the winking of your eyes, the smiles, frowns, sweat and heat generated while conversing. Couples need to pay attention to all these nonverbal cues. Tears communicate the emotions of your spouse. It is not just water coincidentally running down the face of your spouse.

> *Abiola is a Nigerian married to Salisu who is from Gambia. The couple lives in Italy. When it comes to nonverbal communication this is what Salisu says, "When I roll my tongue, it means I am flirting with you, but to Abiola that is teasing. There are so many*

*things we are directly opposite in due to our cultural and country differences. We are still studying each other's signs and body language."*

*Abiola says, "When I am with my sister Fatima, we can do so many things with our eyes, feet and even our noses. A touch on my face or nose means something and we are on our way. I am unable to do the same with Salisu but we are creating our own body language, which is fun."*

It is generally said that females are better at reading body language than males.

*Mary is a Ghanaian living with her boyfriend, Matt. She said, "When it comes to reading signs of emotions and body language, Matt is useless. All he understands is shedding tears. He does not get my frowns, my silence and even my groans. He has to be told exactly what he has to do even in the presence of everyone. He says he is not a mind reader. It is sometimes frustrating to tell him all things."*

Can wives teach men to recognise and understand these nonverbal cues?

*"You must pay attention to the feelings and emotions of your spouse; because they are the purest forms of communication. They transcend all languages."*

**UNKNOWN**

## INTERPRETING BODY LANGUAGE

These are the ways to easily interpret body language:

- **Observe Facial Expressions**

All couples should take time and effort to read the expressions on their spouse's faces. Even though there are variations in the interpretation of body language and gestures between cultures, there is almost universal agreement in facial expression. The facial expressions of happiness, sadness, anger and fear are similar throughout the world.

This means that you should not miss the sadness, anger, grief, joy and excitement on their faces. Just be aware that your spouse from time to time shows their mood and any signs of conflict with their eyes, mouth and lips.

That also means your family and friends will also notice this in the face for both of you. They will know if you are truly a happy couple or pretending.

- **The Eye Contact**

In the western culture maintaining eye contact is seen as a sign of interest, connection, and intimacy. In other cultures, this may be a sign of rudeness. It is, however, important that romantic couples do not miss out on the message that the eyes send. Experts believe that when couples are comfortable with each other, their eyes are dilated, as they gaze at each other and even flirt with their eyes. However, when they are anxious, uncomfortable or hiding something, they avoid eye contact. Couples who are open, transparent and intimate are always giving each other welcoming and romantic eyes.

## NOTICE THE GAP BETWEEN YOU

Non-verbal cues are not only about the body language or the frown on the face, they are also about the space between couples when they are spending time together.

When you are eating together, do you sit closer at the table or do you want to be far from him or her?

When couples are emotionally disconnected, there is a big gap between them when sleeping together. When they are walking together, there is no holding of hands or walking side by side. When couples are having issues you can also see from the gap between them when they sit on the sofa to watch television.

It is important that you observe all these so that you can politely enquire from your spouse if everything is okay. If these subtle but important signals are not picked up and addressed quickly, they develop into massive black holes in the relationship.

Because many gestures and body languages are subject to interpretation, naked couples must confirm with their spouses, what they are reading.

> *Matt said to his Pastor, "Mercy thinks I have time to read every sign on her face. I am the only person working in this family. I have to do multiple jobs*

*to put food on the table and pay the bills. When do I get time to stand and gaze at her or read her body language?"*

*Mercy replied, "Should we wait till we have everything before we can care about each other? I am always stressed, having to look after two little children. My husband does not observe anything I am going through. He sleeps with his face to the wall and covers his head with the quilt. It is dead silent in this marriage."*

Pressures can get in the way of marriage but it is important that in the midst of that, you get your spouse by your side. You can handle any pressure better if you have your partner's support. Transparent and intimate couples read the signs and offer support even if their partners are not asking for it.

## OBSERVE YOUR SEXUAL INTIMACY

It is said that when sex is fine in the marriage then it is likely everything else is fine. If sex is not fine, nothing is fine.

In cultures where freedom of speech is impeded or frowned upon as a result of one's gender, status and maturity, those who are disadvantaged develop the habit of using non-verbal communication. These are also used in their sexual desires or romance. For instance, in some cultures, it is not permitted for a woman to verbally request for sex. So women from such cultures may feel shy to discuss sex or ask for it even when they move on from there. It is therefore important for their husbands to understand what their gestures mean.

Such women may easily be misclassified as not romantic because of a lack of verbal expression. However, if the husbands pay attention to their gestures, they will quickly realise such women are very romantic.

## Dean and Sarah

*Dean has been married to Sarah for three years and they both live in London. Sarah was born and raised in Eritrea in Eastern Africa while Dean is white and was born in Manchester.*

*When they came for counselling, Dean expressed shock that Sarah had never initiated sex, never said 'I love you' and hardly expressed her feelings about sex. Dean thinks this is hard work as he has to do everything to make sex happen.*

*But at counselling, this is what Sarah said in response to Dean's concerns, "My culture does not allow me to ask a man for sex. It is only prostitutes that do that."*

*When she was pressed to explain how she requests for sex, her answer was even more interesting. "You see, it is when I use my eyes to flirt with him. Other times, I just use my legs to rub on him. By doing that, I am telling him I want him."*

*When Dean was asked if he understood what Sarah is saying, Dean was once again shocked because he had not taken notice of any such things and was hearing this for the first time.*

In many cultures, discussions or talks that have got to do with sex are considered taboo. They think it is embarrassing and humiliating to talk about it; even though in private, it is fine to talk about it. This means that children brought up in such cultures are afraid or embarrassed to express their sexual desires. It is up to the spouse who is exposed to such liberties to understand and appreciate their non-verbal signals.

One surest way to resolve such an issue is making time to talk about this.

## Emotions and Behaviour

You see, your emotions and feelings are easily expressed through your face, hair, nose, hands and even your skin. Couples who understand their spouses see their negative signals such as fear, stress, anger, sadness, surprise and disgust. This helps you to stop the strain you are putting on them. If these emotions are stirred by conditions or people outside your marital relationship such as friends, work colleagues or extended family members, then your spouse will know how to comfort and pamper you.

If these feelings are those of happiness, excitement and desire which have not yet been verbally expressed, it is a green light for you to do more of whatever you are doing.

## GUIDING YOUR HUSBAND TO RECOGNISE YOUR BODY LANGUAGE

Wives have an advantage in non-verbal cues but that does not make them great communicators. Great communicators use language that their audience will understand. If you always speak in parables and idiomatic expressions, the chance is that your spouse and children may not always understand you.

But one of the best ways of helping your husband to appreciate your nonverbal cues is drawing his attention to what you observe others do in public or among family and friends.

### Obed and Ruth

*Obed and Ruth live in Accra, Ghana and have been married for 4 years. Ruth says, "I draw Obed's attention if I see a lady flirting with a man and ask him if he understands what the lady means. Usually, all I get from him is, 'Women, you read meanings into everything.' Sometimes I will draw his attention if he is having a conversation with someone who is not interested in what he is saying by stepping on his toes to end it. This did not go well the first time. In fact, he screamed that I was hurting him. After we discussed this, he is now watching and observing my reaction or action when he is in public or preaching."*

**CHECKPOINT**

What are some common body language cues used in your country of origin? Take a sheet of paper each. Write the sexual or romantic gestures that you want your spouse to take notice of.

CHAPTER THREE

# Enemies to Couples' Communication

*"A great marriage is not when the 'perfect couple' comes together. It is when an imperfect couple learns to enjoy their differences."*

DAVE MEURER (American Author)

For any relationship to thrive, all man-made and artificial barriers should be totally eradicated to allow the free flow of all forms of communication and interaction.

Factors that help to improve communication among couples have already been discussed. Here, we will discuss things that can hinder communication among married couples.

These include:

1. Misunderstanding our differences
2. Pressure and stress
3. Criticisms
4. Not forgiving each other
5. Lack of appreciation

## MISUNDERSTANDING OUR DIFFERENCES

COLOSSIANS 4:16 (NIV)

*"Let your conversation be always full of grace, seasoned with salt, so that you may know how to answer everyone."*

As a couple, you differ a lot in so many ways. Probably, it is those differences that brought you together. This is because you did not plan to marry another you.

My son looks like me in appearance and character, which is not bad because I am quite a handsome man, really. What rather frustrates me is when I see him exhibiting some of the mistakes I made as a young man. I just can't stand it. I would not be able to marry anyone of that character. This is why I married Phyllis who is completely opposite to who I am. I must admit there are a few things that Phyllis and I have in common but those we don't share are more. One of the many differences we have is the way we communicate. One obvious thing is that she is female and I am male. Psychologists and scientists agree that males and females communicate differently.

### Your Background and Training Affect the Way You Communicate

We were both born in the village and raised there to certain ages. Phyllis left the village to join her parents in the city of Accra, at the age of nine to attend a good school. She went on to attend some of the most prestigious secondary schools in Ghana. I stayed in the village until I was fifteen and joined my father in another town to attend a comprehensive or middle school. From there, by divine orchestration, I attended not so cool secondary schools. Phyllis is an introvert while I am an extrovert.

My communication style was more of survival than posh. Again, being a male child raised in the village, and also being an extrovert placed me in a disadvantageous position with regard to my communication. Phyllis on the other hand was blessed with gentleness, calmness and fluency with a posh accent by virtue of her temperament, education and upbringing.

I have accepted that I am not a fluent and great speaker compared to my wife. She thinks before she says every word. Words mean a lot to her. I am just the opposite. Most often, I speak before I think about it. Then I backpedal and try to do damage control.

If you are brought up in a family that is well educated, and well-to-do, and you live in a noble part of town, you are more likely to speak well.

However, if you are raised in an environment that is free for all, and has a survival-of-the-fittest aura, it will be difficult to be careful in your communication.

Naked couples study each other, talk about what has shaped their communication, and they adapt to each other. You should not try to teach your partner to speak like you. It should be left to him or her to make that call. But if you married the person, then I guess you also liked the way they spoke and communicated with you before marriage.

### Male and Female Differences in Communication

Apart from the above differences, a couple must understand that males and females do not communicate at the same level. Scientists believe that females tend to have verbal centres on both sides of their brain, while males tend to have verbal centres on only the left hemisphere. This is a significant difference. They believe, it is the reason ladies tend to use more words when discussing or describing incidents, a story, person, object, feeling, or place. Men should not be angry that their wives talk a lot and are able to describe scenes and issues better than they do.

Males not only have fewer verbal centres in general but also have less connectivity between their word centres and their memories or feelings. When it comes to discussing feelings, emotions and senses, females tend to have an advantage. No wonder your wife is able to express her emotions and how she feels all the time and you struggle to do the same. It will therefore be unfair for wives to expect their husbands to be as emotional as them.

## Communication Skills & Body Language

Experts believe that the communication centre inside a woman's brain is much larger than the communication centre inside a man's brain. Women are generally better at processing words and using language than men, provided that all other factors are constant. Women pay special attention to words, read between the lines and can notice the body language of people along with their facial expressions in a much better way than men.

Psychologists believe that typically, a woman speaks 25,000 words a day compared with 12,000 by a man. This is equivalent to 250 words and 125 words per minute for females and males respectively. With this in mind, we should not be accusing each other of being talkative or dumb. We are just different in our composition and makeup. Our differences should not create problems if we understand and appreciate each other. In fact, no one is better. We actually complement each other to be complete.

**CHECKPOINT**

How did your background influence the way you talk? Have you ever talked about this with your spouse? List some of the things that shaped your communication.

## STRESS AND PRESSURE PUT A DAMPER ON COMMUNICATION

When we are under pressure or stressed, it affects how we communicate, receive and process information. Pressures from work, long drives or commuting to work, financial difficulties and setbacks such as a loss of a job or loss of a family member seriously affect the way couples respond to each other. Couples who are naked speak about their pressures and seek support. This enormously lessens the burden. When partners are left on their own to face their own challenges and problems, it eventually leads to serious repercussions on the marriage. When people are dealing with stress, they can become poor communicators or irritable resulting in yelling, blaming, holding grudges, keeping secrets, giving the silent treatment, giving ultimatums, and bringing harm to their partners.

If you want to enjoy your partner, help limit or manage their stress better. It will help you yourself, your children and the marriage. When neither of you is stressed, you see the funny side of issues; you reason better, and you become chattier. Stress reduces our visibility, acceptance and friendliness.

> *Kira noted that, "When Phil starts complaining about everything, from the house not being clean enough to children not doing well, I sense something is not going on well at work. All I do is run a bath for him, give him a head and shoulder massage (his favourite) and put the kids to sleep early to give him nice room service."*

Naked couples are usually able to discern quickly what is wrong with their spouses, even way before they tell them. Naked couples are good body language and face readers. They are also emotionally intelligent persons. They can read each other like a newspaper.

## CRITICISMS

*If you want to break your marriage, keep criticising. Criticisms create barriers in communication, but a compliment is a force that draws spouses closer.*

Criticism is a number one communication Killer! If you want to enjoy your spouse and get his or her full attention, you must genuinely avoid unnecessary criticism and complaints. The devil is the accuser of brethren. Do not join forces with him. If you sweeten your language with great and pleasant comments and compliments, very soon you will not only win your spouse back but your friends and family as well.

COLOSSIANS 4:16 (NIV)

*"Let your conversation be always full of grace, seasoned with salt, so that you may know how to answer everyone."*

There is a big difference between criticism and complaining. You can complain to your spouse if you are unhappy with him or her. I will show you what the difference is.

### Criticism vs Complaints

What is criticism? According to the Merriam–Webster dictionary, it is the act of expressing disapproval, and of noting the problems or faults of a person or thing.

To complain on the other hand, is defined as expressing grief, pain, or discontent about something.

Couples should not mistake one for the other. When you are complaining, you are stating what you see as wrong and how that makes you feel. This is usually not harsh and does not attack your spouse or listener. You just want them to listen and make a change. You want to have your friend back without hurting them, even though you may be hurting from their action.

> *Charlie felt sad that Maria, on a few occasions, had remarked about how short he was in stature. One morning, Charlie called Maria. "Honey, I know you love me and will do anything for me. But of late you have made two or three comments about my stature which I want to draw your attention to. When you do that it makes me feel less confident about myself. It also creates doubt in my mind that I am sufficient for you. Is this something you do on purpose or are unaware of?"*

You can see that Charlie has put his concerns out clearly without attacking Maria. If Maria indeed loves Charlie, it is a no-brainer; there is only one action to take. You would expect Maria to be remorseful and apologise unreservedly to Charlie.

### What About Criticism?

When you criticise, you complain, add your emotions and attack the person for doing that to you. Criticism causes pain, hurt and withdrawal. When you criticise, it makes the recipient feel worthless and useless and may cause them to mount a defence. This defence can cause you to increase your attack which can escalate into insults and counter insults. It is not healthy for any relationship.

Let's use Charlie and Maria's case above as an example:

> *Charlie felt sad that Maria, on a few occasions, had remarked about how short he was in stature. One morning, Charlie called Maria. "Maria, I have always suspected that you fancy tall men. I doubt that you really love me. You probably married me because of my money. If I am too short for you why don't you pack and leave? Huh?! You can file for divorce. I am tired of you making fun of my short stature."*

When you criticise your partner that way, what do you expect next? When you make such unproven allegations and attack their character and integrity, do you expect them to sit back and take all that from you? If you are lucky, some people will be quiet, take all that in and later talk to you. But it is also natural for the person to also mount up a defence, hit back and probably hit harder. In conflict management, this is "flooding". You overflow each other with hurtful words.

This can progress to what we call stonewalling. In stonewalling you give each other a cold attitude or silent treatment. At that stage, you don't want to talk to each other for days, if not for weeks. This is because you are both hurting and frustrated with each other. Couples should try at all costs to avoid criticism because it hurts your communication and your marriage.

See what the Bible says about criticism and harsh words:

EPHESIANS 4:31-32 (NLT)

*Get rid of all bitterness, rage, anger, harsh words, and slander, as well as all types of evil behaviour. Instead, be kind to each other, tender-hearted, forgiving one another, just as God through Christ has forgiven you.*

**CHECKPOINT**

List how criticism by your partner makes you feel. Can you and your partner practise how to complain without attacking each other?

## NOT FORGIVING EACH OTHER

*"A good marriage is the union of two good forgivers."*

RUTH BELL GRAHAM
(American Christian author, most well known as the wife of evangelist Billy Graham)

Your relationship benefits greatly if both of you grow in love, and in forgiving each other. If a couple harbours anger, resentment and unforgiveness, they do not only block their communication channel, but they also block their prayers. It breaks the bond between them and tears them apart.

> MATTHEW 6:14-15 (NIV)
> *"For if you forgive other people when they sin against you, your heavenly Father will also forgive you. But if you do not forgive others their sins, your Father will not forgive your sins."*

When two human beings live together in any enclosure, whether friends, couples, lovers or haters, they will step on each other's toes. Usually, this is brushed aside by many people without making a case out of it.

However, for a couple in a sexual relationship, who are in love, this is easily forgiven and the couple moves on whether with or without an apology. Nonetheless, the ability to forgive depends on the one who is offended. Are they forgiving or not?

The Bible says, *"Love does not keep records of wrongs"* 1 Corinthians 13:5b (CEV). However, many people keep records of wrongs. They just can't let go of any wrong done to them. Even if the offender apologises, and offends them another time, they revisit the previous wrong done to them. This kind of behaviour does not only hurt the relationship, it destroys communication between the couple. It puts a damper on their friendship and sex life.

All lovers must understand that when you forgive your partner, you are forgiving yourself. You are in fact setting yourself free from mental and spiritual bondage. You cannot claim to love your partner and not forgive them.

Angels do not marry. Any human being you choose to marry on earth will offend you. It is how you deal with the offence that shows how much you want the relationship. You ought to work on yourself to be able to forgive before you enter into any relationship.

> *Belinda 42, a Ghanaian living in the USA with her husband Mark sent $200 to her mom at home in Ghana without telling Mark. Mark found out when Belinda's mom called to show her gratitude. Mark was not happy about that at all and has since refused to talk to Belinda. Belinda says, "I did not intend to hide this money. I always discuss every remittance to my family with Mark. I have already apologised to Mark but he says he is struggling to forgive me. He has not spoken to me properly for a week."*

If you plan not to forgive your spouse, you are creating a communication barrier between you. Your action simply means you never offend your partner. You are the holy and righteous one. For the sake of your marriage and family ask God to help you to be forgiving.

**CHECKPOINT**

Can you list the things that are difficult for you to forgive when your spouse offends you?

## LACK OF APPRECIATION FOR YOUR SPOUSE

PROVERBS 16:24 (NLT)
*"Kind words are like honey, sweet to the soul and healthy for the body."*

JOB 4:4 (NLV)
*"Your words have helped him*
*stand who would have fallen.*
*You have given strength to weak knees."*

How do you feel when your spouse fails to notice your good deeds? How often do you also step back and acknowledge what your spouse does for you? How do you feel when your husband or wife takes time to appreciate you for what you do? And how do you think they will also feel if you also appreciate them?

When you appreciate the little things your partner does for you, it boosts their morale and gives them extra energy to do even more.

Appreciation is best defined by the Cambridge dictionary as follows:

> *"The act of recognising someone's worth as a person, or showing that you are grateful for something that person has done."*

When you show appreciation, you are telling your partner that you are grateful; that you are thankful, and that you are completely satisfied with him or her. You acknowledge that you are totally indebted to them for all their sacrifices. You are in effect saying, "You deserve my tribute and recognition!"

The opposite is also true if you do not appreciate your partner. They become worried and tell themselves the following: My wife or husband is probably not satisfied or happy with me. Then in their heart, they will begin to harbour resentment against you. They will call you all sorts of names but you will not hear. They will think you are rude and ungrateful. You might not be an ungrateful person except that you have not prioritised this. But life is all about meeting expectations. You may have many big plans for your partner tomorrow or in the future, but how will they know? Naked couples are able to put aside their own demands, expectations and pressures, and find good times and best places and the right times to say 'thank you' to their spouses.

## How to Appreciate Your Partner Properly

### Thank You

The expression 'thank you' can be so powerful and have a great effect on your spouse if you choose the right place, right moments, and the right tone to say it. Simply put, say it like you genuinely mean it. The love and tone in your voice, your facial expression and your proximity to your spouse will make him or her feel so special.

> *Mike 41 from London passed by the local shop after work and bought chocolate for £2 and put it in his pocket. He went straight to the kitchen where Lena was cooking and at the same time looking after their 1-year-old son. He pulled Lena tight to himself, looked straight into her face as if he wanted to give her a kiss and whispered, "Lena, I am in awe of you. You look after Jack each day, all by yourself and you still manage to cook and do other household chores, every day! I don't know how you manage this. But once again, I want to say thank you. This is a token for you to share with me."*
>
> *Lena said she was close to tears, hearing this from Mike. This is what Lena said, "He says thank you all the time but this one felt so special. It made me feel that someone appreciates me, even though I do not go to work."*

Whether it is a flower, chocolate or a big present you buy to say thank you, it still matters how you say it. You don't have to do it in a hurry. If time is not on your side, please wait and do it properly.

It is important to understand that both men and women want to be appreciated. Don't always wait for your spouse to say I am grateful for your hard work then you give feedback, 'Me too'. Please find your own time and space to express your gratitude.

Men may not need chocolate or flowers but it is important you make them feel valued.

> *This is how Aysha showed her gratitude to David. "You always come home with a smile on your face. You never complain about all the bills you pay. I feel I am the luckiest wife. For this, I am truly grateful."*
>
> *This was David's response, "As a man, you never expect to be appreciated. You just have to do what you can to support your wife and family. For Aysha to take the time and effort to do that was priceless. I feel very motivated to do even more for her and the family. Thank you, Aysha."*

Every thank you is good but it is even better if you don't batch all the lot together. Take your time and say them one after the other.

### When do you say it?

It is important that you don't wait until Christmas or a special occasion to say thank you. Each day, you should be able to find at least three things to be thankful for. I am sure the men will have several things to thank their wives for. Appreciate their bodies, curves, hairstyle, modesty, the meals they cook, doing household chores, looking after the children, keeping your bedroom, etc.

I am sure the ladies will also have something to say as well: Playing with the kids, buying stuff from stores, paying bills, receiving visitors, receiving your family when they visit, dad's taxi, gardening, fixing things around the house, etc.

So, you see, there are a countless number of things that you can appreciate your husband or wife for.

**CHECKPOINT**

Can you think of three things about your partner that you are grateful for and let them know how grateful you are for those things? What reaction are you expecting from him or her?

CHAPTER FOUR

# The Power of Affection

*Kind words are appreciated by everyone irrespective of our culture and background. Kind words are golden. They are warmth to the heart of your partner.*

Affection simply means the gentle feeling of fondness or liking. Naked couples are very comfortable showing affection to each other.

There are several ways we can show affection: hugging, kissing, touching, cuddling, words of affirmation and endearment. But to certain ladies, affection means the following: helping to do house chores, washing up, taking the bin out and standing in the kitchen with them. This means affection can mean different things to different people.

You see, when you have feelings of fondness for your partner, you want to hold them, touch them, kiss them and say kind words to them. Affection does not only enhance communication, it also increases bonding between the couple.

There are however certain cultures where affection is not encouraged in public.

I have seen many African couples in Europe and elsewhere constantly quarrelling about their partners not showing them affection the same way white couples do. Some people think that when couples are in Rome, they should do what the Romans do.

How do culture and traditions affect the way we communicate our affection? Do Africans have to communicate their affection the same way as our white counterparts?

## CULTURE AND PUBLIC DISPLAY OF AFFECTION

Western cultures permit demonstration of affection in public spaces. They do so without any struggle. They would kiss, hug and hold hands. Most cultures permit the holding of hands in the public space. However, they will frown on couples hugging and kissing in public. Do such cultures draw people back?

> *Mary and Vinnie are married and live in Kampala, Uganda. They have been married for 10 years. Mary says "As for Vinnie, the only time he will touch me is when he wants sex. Even though we are both educated and watch romantic films he will never practise what we watch. I want us to practise what we see."*
>
> *Vinnie agrees with Mary but has some reservations. "You see, no one in our neighbourhood does that.*

*Our parents never do that. What do you think people will take us for if we start doing that?"*

This does not only happen on the continent, when couples travel abroad they have this dilemma. One part wants to be affectionate and romantic in public and private whilst the other part may find it unacceptable.

*Vicky is a 40-year old Ghanaian and a medical doctor living with Paul in London. Vicky dragged Paul to the counsellor for one reason: "Paul is neither romantic nor affectionate." When asked to elaborate this is what she said, "It is a pity that Paul walks ahead of me in public. He never holds my hands, and will never kiss me in public. The last time I asked for a kiss at the bus stop, he flared up and embarrassed me."*

*Paul defended his action and said, "I cannot take it anymore from her. Vicky has completely changed. She thinks I should be like her white male friends who show affection in public. I have told her that as a Ghanaian, I am not used to this and it will not happen."*

Married couples should aim at pleasing no one except each other. Marriage should be based on love and friendship. Love does not demand what one wants. You negotiate with your partner and settle for a middle ground. When a couple moves or relocates to another town or country, they should agree on which cultural values they want to maintain and which ones they would like to adopt. No one should be made to feel inferior, insufficient or guilty for not following someone else's culture.

Some people refuse to marry from other cultures because they do not agree with their practices. So, you should be careful not to dwell too much on what someone is doing. You should not copy blindly. Appreciate your cultures and traditions, and negotiate with your spouse what you want to adopt.

CHECKPOINT

Can you list some of the practices you want to adopt in your marriage which are not usually done in your country of origin?

**WORDS OF ENDEARMENT**

Phyllis and I were living in Ghana when we got married. We agreed to use some words of endearment for each other. We still do. But I quickly realised that my wife loved it when I called her Amma. And I loved her response, "Papa". That means 'Daddy'. We are not ashamed to call each other by that in public because that is what we call ourselves when at home. I have realised that many of our followers have also adopted these same words of endearment.

A wife of a pastor friend told me she hates it when her husband mounts the pulpit and refers to her with all sweet names as if he is loving and affectionate.

> *Martha complained, "He would never say good morning to me, never touch me and never say 'I love you' unless he wants sex. My husband is a hypocrite."*

Words of endearment such as 'babe', 'honey',' toffee', 'sweetie' and the likes are common in the cities and the western world. Some spouses hate to be referred to as certain objects. It is important to discuss with your spouse if they are cool with it before you start calling them. And ask if they will be happy to be called such names in public as well.

'I love you' is powerful and most men and women really love it. My wife says she can never have enough of I love you. She loves it in the morning, evening, day and night. She will appreciate it in all weather and seasons. She will appreciate it in the kitchen, bathroom, bedroom and in public.

I love you is not foreign per se but where it is said might be a bit challenging for shy spouses.

### HUGGING AND KISSING

Many cultures in Africa, Asia and the Middle East may find this too intimate for public consumption. I never saw my parents doing this even at home let alone in public. Phyllis and I do it though in the presence of our children, not that they appreciate it as they grow older. But I will not be comfortable doing that in public. I will not be surprised if my children who have been raised in the UK decide to go a step further than us.

All these are governed by your culture, traditions, values and religion. Your actions and behaviours have been shaped by this important part of your lives.

## TOUCHING EACH OTHER INCREASES BONDING AND AFFECTION

Physical touch is a powerful tool in communication. It enhances emotional connection and gets your spouse's attention.

It has long been known that physical touch is a way of communicating emotional love. Numerous research projects in the area of child development have reached the conclusion that: **Babies who are held, hugged, and kissed develop a healthier emotional life than those who are left for long periods of time without physical contact**. Physical touch is also a powerful vehicle for increasing bonding and affection with our partners.

> *Megan, a teacher married to Victor has this to say, "When Victor and I have not touched each other for three days or more, it feels like we are just housemates. We drift completely apart from each other. But when we are showing affection, he is on my mind even at work."*

Marriage can be very costly. No wonder Apostle Paul gave the counsel that if it is possible, let people stay unmarried!

Do not enter into marriage with unrealistic expectations from your spouse. Be aware that marriage is service and hard work and must come from both sides.

It takes two to make the marriage successful but it takes one to make it a failure.

**CHECKPOINT**

Are you comfortable praising or touching your partner in public? If not, is it because your culture or religion frowns upon it?

## SUGAR EACH OTHER WITH KIND WORDS

*Instead of making your spouse tear up with unkind words, make them cry with laughter and with kind words.*

Kind words are appreciated by everyone irrespective of our culture and background. Kind words are golden. They are warmth to the heart of your partner. When you possess the ability to find positives even in a dire situation, even kings will seek your service and pay for it. It is not hard to melt the heart of your husband or wife. Each day, find something nice to tell them. Do that consistently for about three weeks and you will see a massive transformation in your love life.

This is usually in private. But it can be in public as well. I see many men of God praising their wives from the pulpit all the time. It is a beautiful thing to do so far as they are also doing the same in their private spaces. It will be disappointing and hypocritical to show off in church or in public but bully each other in your closets.

> *"In the silence of night, I have often wished*
> *for just a few words of love from one man,*
> *rather than the applause of thousands of people."*
> *Judy Garland (American actress and singer.)*

## What Does the Bible Say About Kind Words?

> PROVERBS 15:23 (NLT)
> *"Everyone enjoys a fitting reply;*
> *it is wonderful to say the right*
> *thing at the right time!"*

> PROVERBS 16:24 (NLT)
> *"Kind words are like honey*
> *—sweet to the soul and*
> *healthy for the body."*

How would you feel hearing statements like these from your partner?

> "You are so special to me and I cannot afford
> to lose you."

"My life has been complete since you arrived."

"I feel so satisfied with your presence;
I don't know what life would have been without you."

"You are an amazing husband or wife;
I feel so lucky to have you."

"Your love is so irresistible;
I am sticking with you forever."

*Abigail says, "Tom seems to find the right kind of words to say to me, especially when I have served him or cooked for him. It does not just make me want to do more for him but it makes me feel special. It makes me feel I am important to him. He is just so kind with his praise."*

**CHECKPOINT**

List 3 things you want to practise with your spouse to affirm your love and romance, especially in public.

List 3 things you find unacceptable to do with your spouse in public

PART

# 3

# Money Matters in Marriage

*"A feast is made for laughter, wine makes life merry, and money is the answer for everything."*

Ecclesiastes 10:19 (NIV)

*"But people who long to be rich fall into temptation and are trapped by many foolish and harmful desires that plunge them into ruin and destruction. For the love of money is the root of all kinds of evil. And some people, craving money, have wandered from the true faith and pierced themselves with many sorrows."*

1 Timothy 6:9-10 (NIV)

# Introduction

The aim of this section is to:

1. Make couples understand the reasons they have differing views on how to manage family income.
2. Draw the attention of the husband and wife to reasons why there is financial secrecy, dishonesty and mismanagement in their relationship.
3. Highlight the differences in perception of financial management between a man and a woman, and how conditions such as location affect their attitude towards their finance.

It is in the interest of couples to work together to bring financial fidelity into their relationship to enjoy the benefits of a great marriage. I have suggested a number of guidelines to follow to achieve this.

CHAPTER ONE

# Money: Its Power and Control in Marriage

If your name were Money, you would be the most talked about and sought after person in the world! You would be everyone's friend. In fact, the entire world would follow your Twitter feeds. You would be the most famous person on earth. Governments, kings, presidents, ladies and gentlemen would be at your beck and call, day and night!

Economists think money is the agent that makes the world go round. Its absence is like trying to drive a brand new car without fuel. Any marriage lacking money can be compared to driving a car without fuel.

Another group of people also have a firm belief that regardless of your nationality, race, educational background, or whether you are physically challenged or not, once you are wealthy, you will attract the most beautiful ladies you want! They think money is such a powerful magnet that every man should have.

My grandfather used to tell me that 'money is blood' and that without it, a man is as good as dead. When you have money, not only does everyone love you; in fact, they consider you a blood brother or sister even if you are not in any way related to them! He used to tell me that a man who has no money loses the respect of his wife and society.

King Solomon puts it better in Ecclesiastes 9:16 (NLT):

> *"So even though wisdom is better than strength,*
> *those who are wise will be despised if they are poor.*
> *What they say will not be appreciated for long."*

Such is the importance and power of money in our modern society. Let's dig a bit deeper to see how the influence of money affects the marital relationship.

## DOES MONEY ANSWER ALL THINGS?

The Bible through King Solomon confirms that Money answers all things.

> ECCLESIASTES 10:19 (NIV)
> *"A feast is made for laughter,*
> *wine makes life merry, and money*
> *is the answer for everything."*

If money answers all things, then you will agree it is reasonable that both men and women travel across the globe in search of money. People move from villages into cities, from one country to another to earn more money to improve their livelihood.

If you live in certain countries in Africa, you can only have good medical care when you are rich. You can access the best education for your children only when you are rich. Some people believe that you can even 'buy' the law with money. You can also have access to the president of a country and get contracts signed within minutes if you are wealthy. Money does not only give you wings to fly, it also gives you control and power!

No wonder many people have sacrificed their morals and have acted contrary to their values because stashes of cash were put before them. People who do not deserve certain positions have managed to acquire them just because they paid someone money. Again, because of money, certain ladies have also accepted marriage proposals from certain men they did not love. Similarly, many opportunistic men have also married many women they will never love. There are so many gold hunters out there; it is so difficult to tell who is genuinely in love with you, especially if one is rich or famous.

So long as we dwell on earth, money will always be key to opening many great doors. For this same reason, money will always be one of the most difficult issues in marriages. Therefore, all couples, especially the young ones, will need to be aware of the devastating effect of money, either the lack of it or the love of it, and mount up effective strategies to protect their marriages.

## THE NO-MONEY-NO-MARRIAGE SYNDROME

In many cultures in Africa and Asia, parents and families play a huge role in young couples' marriages. Regardless of the ages of the couple wanting to marry, parents or family heads must still give consent before the marriage can be contracted. Unfortunately, due to poverty, some families feel obliged to ensure that the man has a stable income before he can marry their daughter. There must be evidence that the young man has a good job to bring in the money or a stash of cash or many cows to give to the family before they are given the chance to negotiate with family heads for marriage to be contracted.

When financial demands are satisfied, they proceed to do checks on the following as well:

- Tribe compatibilities
- Family compatibilities
- Presence of any chronic diseases in either family
- Psychological or neurological disorders

You may question whether these checks ensure that couples love each other but in such cultures, love is not the ultimate reason to get married. Rather, the family of the bride-to-be are mostly more concerned about the man being able to take care of their daughter. This means that marriages are driven more by money than love. The woman's marriage is considered by the family as the route to financial freedom for the family.

There are a few reasons why this happens.

Firstly, there are no social benefits or government support for many countries and families. It is therefore critical for the ladies and their families to ensure that anyone marrying their daughters has a guaranteed source of income.

Secondly, families demand huge bride prices in certain cultures as though their daughter is for sale. If a man cannot afford the bride price, it is assumed that he will not be able to take good care of the lady when he marries her. They consider your ability to pay a bride price as a show of your masculinity.

Thirdly, they consider good husbands to be breadwinners. Women in such cultures are supposed to look up to their husbands for money to take care of the home and the children. Men who cannot afford to look after their wives and families lose respect in society.

For those reasons, when a gentleman shows interest in a young lady, the family investigates and interrogates if he has the financial power to marry.

> *Sam 25 is working with Vodafone as a site manager in Ghana. He visited Sue 23, his fiancée for the second time in her parent's home. Sam borrowed his friend's posh VW Tiguan while paying Sue this visit. This is because Sue's parents were not very receptive the first time Sam visited. He went by public transport and was not smartly dressed on the first visit. This time, he wore a nice suit, and a tie to match. He also bought Sue's parents some foodstuff. Can you imagine the reaction of the parents towards Sam this time around?*

> *Before Sam left, Sue's mom came and asked with a cheerful smile, "So when are you guys planning for the engagement?" Before Sam could say a word, Dad also added with a smile, "There is no need to wait any longer." He further added, "I can see how beautiful your marriage will be."*

So, this is the reality of the power and influence money can have on relationships among certain cultures. Luckily, couples in western countries do not face this because jobs, cars and medical care are considered a basic necessity and almost everyone has them anyway. But can you understand that if parents played a key role in securing a rich husband for their daughter, they will then demand a share of the cake from their daughter?

I am sure you might have heard the phrase "cows are coming home."When one gives birth to a girl, there is a great celebration because someone will one day marry her and the bride price can range from 2 cows to 20 cows.

If families give their daughters into marriage as if the man is purchasing a commodity, do you expect him to treat her as an equal partner?

For we know that where there is no sense of equality, there will be no respect and transparency. Simply put, if the foundation of our marriage is bedevilled with family orchestration to gain financial freedom for themselves and the bride, financial transparency or nakedness will be compromised.

*Tina complained to the counsellor, "I have no idea how much Tom earns even though we have been married for 5 years. I have no idea how he spends his money; yet, he wants me to show him how I spend my money because he pays the rent. It will not happen! I am holding onto my money. After all, it is he who married me and it is his responsibility to look after the home. My money is my money, period."*

## WHAT IS FINANCIAL NAKEDNESS?

Financial nakedness is when a couple in a relationship is so committed to each other that their money, wealth and possessions are considered joint property. The way they earn and spend money is no secret and there is no fear or suspicion that one will abuse this trust. The one who earns more money does not hide a portion from the other who earns less. The one who earns less also brings all that they earn to the table. No one feels inferior and no one feels superior. Income or expenditures are as clear as crystals. Bank checks, bank statements, payslips and internet banking details including passwords are fully shared. At any time, both are aware of the bank balances. Husband and wife are comfortable with each other's spending and savings. They have agreed on ways of paying the mortgage or rent and bills. Each person still has the autonomy to treat themselves to new things and to give out or donate without fear of reprisal. Couples' assets, insurances and wills are all open to both or are jointly done.

Remittances to their family and friends have been agreed on and there is no need to hide anything.

Such couples have gained ascendency over money so much that it is no longer a threat to their relationship.

Money is no longer the root cause of any evil in their marriage. These are what I term as financial nakedness. If you have reached this height, you deserve to pat yourselves on the back. In fact, you deserve a huge medal. Couples who are honest with their finances will enjoy other great benefits in marriage such as friendship, quality time, affection and sex.

**CHECKPOINT**

What part did MONEY play in choosing your partner?

List 5 other things that influenced your choice?

CHAPTER TWO

# Six Key Factors That Influence Couples' Financial Transparency

*"Don't love money; be satisfied with what you have. For God has said, 'I will never fail you. I will never abandon you'."*

HEBREWS 13:5 (NLT)

*"Money cannot buy peace of mind. It cannot heal ruptured relationships, or build meaning into a life that has none."*

RICHARD M. DEVOS
(was an American billionaire businessman, co-founder of Amway and owner of the Orlando Magic basketball team)

The willingness and desire to be open and transparent in the financial matters of your marriage depends on several factors that have shaped your thinking and experience. These factors include:

1. Background of the couple
2. The breadwinner superiority
3. When the unemployed gains employment
4. Unforgiving couples
5. Adapting to changes in the couple's circumstances
6. Accountability to each other

## BACKGROUND OF THE COUPLE

Couples' background and culture ultimately affect their transparency or lack of it. Where you grew up, the traditions of the people, the culture and history of such environment shape you. You develop your opinions and perception from what you were told from childhood and what you observed. If parents themselves are fair and transparent with each other, they transfer these values to their children advertently or inadvertently.

Similarly, if you were raised in a family or society, where all things are shrouded in mystery, superstitions and secrecy, you are most likely to be influenced by those values.

Differences in the background of couples in nurturing and training can disturb your marriage. Naked couples appreciate their differences and shortcomings due to their nurturing and make a conscious effort to adapt to the changes in circumstances. When any of the couples involved in such relationships are not willing to be flexible, their marriage will encounter great difficulties.

*Paul 34, married to Linda 29, said "I do not understand all the fuss about financial transparency. I worked hard to earn my money. If Linda also works hard, her money belongs to her. I am the man, I have an obligation to look after my family. I will not share my responsibility. My dad will not be proud of me if he hears I am not looking after my wife."*

Paul says in his Igbo land in Nigeria, men have to be men. Your power as a man is your money. "If you show all your money to your wife, you are doomed! You must keep your wife guessing how much you earn. That is how you earn her respect", he stressed.

So you can see that Paul's origin plays a key role in how he handles his money in their marriage. When they lived in Nigeria, both Paul and Linda never questioned the practice. But since they moved to New York, Linda wants more transparency.

Linda and Paul must both accept to change or stick to their cultural practices to maintain harmony in the home. If it is only Linda who wants a change without first appreciating Paul's stance, this will affect the stability of the marriage.

## THE BREADWINNER SUPERIORITY

The breadwinner is the one who earns money and provides for the family's needs. The word is very 'western' because, in my African culture, bread is not a major food. I can agree with 'salsa winner', 'fufu winner' or 'eba winner'; whatever staple food is in your culture.

I know some breadwinners who consider their monies as family income but the majority feel superior and lack openness to the partner who does not earn any income. Those who do not earn income quietly obey the breadwinner.

In the past, men and women accepted that as their roles and responsibilities. Husbands worked hard and brought the money; the wife respected and served the husband so that he felt good. If the woman needed money to keep the home, she just asked her husband. Obviously, such a relationship usually lacked not just transparency, but also mutual respect. This is because the breadwinner felt superior to the one who earned little or nothing. But when there is genuine love in the marriage, couples should share all their money and wealth with love without making their partners feel inferior nor feeling superior in themselves. What about one day when the tides are turned, how will you expect to be treated?

Look at how Jesus commanded:

> MATTHEW 6:31 (NET)
> *"Treat others in the same way*
> *that you would want them to treat you."*

**WHEN THE UNEMPLOYED GAINS EMPLOYMENT**

When the husband and wife are employed or earning income, it is supposed to ease off financial pressure in the family. It is also a time to increase bonding and transparency among couples. However, this can also create discontentment, disunity and lack of transparency. This happens if the one who is now employed feels his or her partner was not fair or transparent when they were not employed. This has affected many marriages and families leading to conflicts and separations. No situation is ever permanent, so if you are the employed partner, be careful how you treat your unemployed spouse. You are setting the tone for fairness, togetherness and transparency or lack of them.

**CHECKPOINT**

If you were not employed at any time in your relationship, list the reasons you were unemployed? How did this period affect transparency in your marriage?

## UNFORGIVING COUPLES

A great marriage is when two sinners are prepared to let go and forgive each other because of the irresistible love between them. Lack of transparency is manifested hugely in warring and unforgiving couples. When couples are not willing to forgive each other the first thing they do is protect their money. They quickly put a lid on their financial chest as if money is the ultimate in marriage. But great couples are those who are quick to forgive each other. They are also quick to say sorry.

Such couples accept they are after all both human and fallible! They understand that Christ forgave them whilst they were liars, thieves, adulterers and enemies of God.

I love how Apostle Paul says it:

> ROMAN 5:8 (NIV)
> *"But God demonstrates his own love for us in this: While we were still sinners, Christ died for us."*

So couples' love is made perfect when they forgive each other without paying each other back in their own coin.

## ADAPTING TO CHANGES IN COUPLES' CIRCUMSTANCES

Life is dynamic and so is marital life. Your marriage is a long journey that will travel with you through the years.

You are going to go through many changes and circumstances. Some of them are positive and pleasant whilst others will be sour and unpleasant. The foundation and principles of openness and honesty will be rattled along the way with these changes.

> *Rita, a nurse and a mother of three said this about her husband "Joe was loving and caring. Above all, he was very transparent and honest with money. I earned far more than him as a nurse and he was an account officer. I could not pursue my career with great ambition with three kids but he did. Since he started earning 5-figure sums, his payslips, bank statements and internet baking details are no longer available. He covers and hides all his income and expenditures. I feel I am the next target he will get rid of."*

The law of change states that nothing stays the same over time. That means your circumstance will change; your body and health will change. Your financial situation will also change.

In fact, your location may also change. You may move from a house, town or country usually in search of greener pastures. All this will require your action to stabilise the relationship. Naked couples talk and discuss possible foreseeable changes and find ways of limiting their negative impact on their relationship. Will you both be fair and transparent to each other in all these changes?

### The Principle of Equilibrium

Think about how the old arrangement between husband and wife worked for both of them like a see-saw. If the weight on both sides is the same, there is no movement until someone adds more weight to one side. Then you see it swing in one direction.

This system remained steady and stable in that equilibrium until one of the factors keeping it in equilibrium changed. This is similar to what my chemistry teacher taught me about Le Chatelier's Principle of equilibrium of gases. Let me quote it here for the sake of those who do not have any idea.

> *"When any system at equilibrium for a*
> *long period of time is subjected to a change*
> *in concentration, temperature, volume, or pressure,*
> *the system changes to a new equilibrium, and this*
> *change partly counteracts the applied change."*

This simply means that when a settled system is disturbed, it will adjust to diminish the change that has been made to it.

In marriage, the change may not be concentration, temperature, volume or pressure but it can be any of the following:

1. Instigation by friends
2. Environmental changes such as migration
3. New income stream for the non-earner
4. Education for a previously uneducated partner, etc.

It is when couples do not react positively and timely to this new change that it poses a lot of problems for the marriage. So when any of the factors keeping the system in a state of equilibrium changes, couples have to re-adjust to offset the new changes.

What it means is that, if previously you did not show your partner your income, now that you are also earning, you must show them your income.

If previously you never helped to pay rent, you might want to consider paying rent now that you are earning. It is that simple.

These changes will be a test of your honesty and transparency. They may predict the longevity, financial blessings and happiness of your marriage.

## ACCOUNTABILITY TO EACH OTHER

One secret to successful financial transparency in your marriage is accepting that you are accountable to your partner.

This has got nothing to do with gender, race or status. Couples are partners, and partnership brings about responsibility and accountability to each other. If you do not become accountable, you are either disrespecting your spouse or undermining the power and strength of the partnership.

When couples are having problems, it is usually because either both or one of them is refusing to be accountable. Couples' desire and determination to be accountable to each other in financial matters influence the transparency and success of the marriage.

**CHECKPOINT**

Which of the factors above are easily having an effect on your financial transparency? Discuss any factors which are not mentioned here with your spouse.

CHAPTER THREE

# Financial Management in Modern Marriage

*"Suppose one of you wants to build a tower, won't you first sit down and estimate the cost to see if you have enough money to complete it."*

LUKE 14:28 (NIV)

Many couples struggle a great deal with how to manage their finances because no one is taught how to manage money before marriage!

When only one person is earning income, how does that affect the marriage dynamics? If both husband and wife are earning income, how do they manage their finances? Is there one format or solution that fits all that needs to be followed?

Who should pay the bills, rent or mortgage? Who should buy food for the home? And who should buy clothes for the kids? If we are immigrants, how do we ensure that we have enough money to acquire property in our country of origin? This and many more such questions bring about confusion and pressure on many marriages.

Couples should find time and space to talk about these issues without their emotions getting in the way to ensure that there is financial nakedness and proper management in the marriage.

**NEW WAYS OF MANAGING FAMILY FINANCES**

Some old British folks I work with tell me their fathers used to work hard and at the end of the month, they would give all their income minus their transport fare to their wives to take care of the home. The wives decided what shirt or trousers to buy for their husbands. The wives also used some of the money to buy stuff for the children and ensured that everyone was well taken care of. She kept the home clean and tidy and ensured she looked after herself well. She did not just spend the money; she ensured there was a reserve for savings. The wife was not just the home manager but also, the financial manager.

They told me that so far as the woman was managing the money, there was total peace! When I asked if he does the same today, he said, "no, my wife works, why should I give all my money to her?" He quizzed. Couples must adapt to new situations and circumstances just like my friend above. Life is very dynamic! Couples' marriage and life must truly reflect this.

## EDUCATION AND JOB – EQUALITY, CHALLENGES IN THE MARRIAGE

When both husband and wife are well educated and gainfully employed, conditions set in their marriage are always different. This is true whether they live in the village, town, city or abroad.

Couples in that situation may have to redefine spousal responsibilities in the marriage.

These include:

i. Who should do the house chores?
ii. Who should do the cooking?
iii. Who should look after the children?
iv. Who should pay for the rent and bills?
v. How should we manage our money?
vi. Should the man still enjoy his authority?
vii. How should the wife be helped at home?

A job and money give the spouse power to negotiate and share duties

### New Paradigm Shift

1. Women are now very educated. Modern society has more women who are very intelligent and well educated. Women head many corporations and countries. They are therefore financially independent of men.
2. The world now accepts women are extremely intelligent to make their own decisions. It is the period that no woman can be dictated to. They have the right to decide what is best for them. Your wife is in this same bracket.

3. Women can do whatever men can do. Some people even go further to state that whatever a man can do, a woman can do it better. It is one of the realities of life that some men find difficult to accept. It is said that when I was little, I would cry if a girl scored higher marks in class than me.
4. A woman's place is no more in the kitchen. The kitchen is a place for everyone; children, adults, girls or boys, men and women and not just wives. You cannot be hard on your wife if food is not ready after work. She is probably not at home by the time you come home from work. You might as well find something to cook and leave some for her.
5. Women are clever at management at every level. They manage the home, the office and even countries. There is no limitation to what they can achieve. They are capable of managing their own money and resources.
6. Men do not know it all. If men know it all, so do women. But nobody knows it all anyway. Don't be deceived because your wife probably knows more about you than you know about yourself and your family.
7. Men are not necessarily supermen. In fact, nobody is. You have your flaws and so does your wife. But the two of you should complement each other in your marriage.
8. Men can also be involved in household chores. If you need your wife to support you with money and pay for the bills, it is fair not to leave all household chores to her.
9. Men can be involved in the training and upbringing of children. Wives were unofficially given the responsibility

of children trainers. Fathers did not show too much interest because their wives were home. This should now be a shared responsibility.

10. Men can also be househusbands. It is okay not to have as great a job as your wife. It is okay to stay home and look after the kids if your wife is earning a 5-figure income.
11. Both husband and wife do earn money. It is great for the family if the husband and wife are working. Accept that this is the norm. The wife should not depend on her husband for pocket money every time.
12. Husband and wife complement each other. This is the beauty of marriage, that we are not just husband and wife; we are like 'lock and key', we make each other tick.
13. Wives understand their home is where they live with their husbands and children. Wives are now building their own families outside their family of origin. They now support their husbands more than ever. This is a win-win for the marriage.
14. It is now okay for the wife to pay for the mortgage or rent if she can afford it. Previously, a woman in certain cultures will be ridiculed for being a breadwinner or for paying rent and bills. This belongs to the past. Women now do whatever it takes to support their own families.
15. Your monies belong to you both. There is now no differentiation between husbands' and wives' money. They both earn and spend as fit for the family.

**CHECKPOINT**

What are some of the things you and your partner are still struggling with? What is your arrangement at home regarding chores and financial commitment?

## FAMILY SAVINGS MANAGEMENT

PROVERBS 10:4 (NIV)

*"Lazy hands make for poverty,*
*but diligent hands bring wealth."*

Be a slave to the love of money, and be spiritually bankrupt.

### There Is Pressure On Our Income

Whether you live in Lagos, Accra, London or New York, your income is under immense pressure. You have a responsibility to manage it well to ensure you do not go bankrupt. Most families have just one or two sources of income which is steady and stable each month. But you have many bills, rent and other subscriptions to pay each month. You have your car, travel and transport to take care of. You have birthdays, Christmas presents and other social commitments as well. Some of you might have to remit your parents and family members home and abroad. If you are a Christian, you have a commitment to the church as well. You will be required to give tithes, offerings and other offerings. All this will come from the same static income you earn each month.

### Planning Your Family Finances

This is the reason why it is important for couples to have a strong financial planning mentality to have surplus income each month. Hard money earned should not be wasted on things you do not actually need. If you want to have spare cash, plan your income and expenditure well to avoid impulse purchases.

The Bible talks seriously about planning so Christians have no excuse.

> LUKE 14:28 (NIV)
>
> *"Suppose one of you wants to build a tower.*
> *Won't you first sit down and estimate the cost*
> *to see if you have enough money to complete it."*

Unfortunately, many African couples do not plan well for savings, retirement and pensions. That lack of planning is likely to affect a couple's income. If you are married, I recommend that you both have a financial coach just as you have a spiritual coach who is usually your pastor or church leader or imam. Have a plan in place to save a good percentage of your income and make every effort to reduce unnecessary expenditures.

Lack of financial planning has resulted in conflicts in many African homes. When there is a lack of a clearly defined plan for the family, everyone assumes they can use their earned monies anyhow.

It will be very useful if husbands or the family develop a roadmap that is clear and concise for both husband and wife to follow. The percentage of your salary to be saved has to be agreed on based on your earnings.

But don't wait until you earn six-figure sums before you start saving. You see, if there is no plan for savings towards say, a mortgage, a holiday, children's education, or retirement, then it is obvious the couple will spend money anyhow.

## Avoid Spending What You Don't Have

One dangerous trap for many couples is spending the money they don't have. A credit card is not free money. It has huge interest you have to pay. Disciplined couples use credit cards but they have set themselves up to pay them off as soon as possible. If you let the credit card balance build up, you are going to be in trouble. Avoiding over-reliance on credit facilities should be part of your financial planning.

If your income is stable then you have to manage your expenditure well before you can get any decent savings.

## HAVING A MINDSET OF SAVING

*Savings = Income minus expenditure*

What the above equation means is that if you want to raise your savings or spare income, you can do two things:

1. **Raise your income.** Work hard or have multiple jobs. Sell on eBay, Amazon, etc, and/or

2. **Reduce your expenditure.** Check where you are haemorrhaging money. Make a conscious effort to reduce utility bills, TV subscriptions, credit card balances and impulse purchases.

Many Africans live in poverty because saving is not well practised. The culture of 'hand to mouth' has a negative outcome on the family. When there are no savings, couples struggle in times of adversity such as job losses, chronic sickness, accidents and any eventuality which prevents them from working for some time or permanently.

Europeans are very good with savings. They are taught to start saving from childhood. Every UK household has savings of some sort. This is either for their children or for parents themselves. It is a culture that all Africans living at home or abroad must adopt.

Most Africans look at their salary and straight away they are thinking about what they can buy; what they can send home, or what business they can do in Africa.

I have been a victim of all this. I have wasted huge sums of money in Africa while living in the UK. I could have saved such monies for my children or for my retirement.

## Reasons Many African Couples Have Low Savings

It is important that couples are prudent in their expenditure if they want to save some money. Money can be very tight for Africans working in cities and abroad.

According to the Office of National Statistics (ONS) in the UK, median household disposable income in the UK was £29,400 in the Financial Year Ending (FYE) 2019. Household income includes all money from Mum, Dad and children. If your household income is £25,000 or more you will get no benefits or income support from the State.

I am aware that many African homes earn more than the UK average household income, yet they struggle to save. They do not have savings and they do not have houses of their own. Reasons for this are many but the top reasons are:

1. Lack of openness in a couple's finances
2. Lack of financial planning by the couple
3. Uncontrolled expenditure
4. Pressure to send money back home
5. Disagreement on individual or joint account
6. Misunderstanding of what a family income is

## Ben and Beth

*Ben is an engineer married to Beth in Nigeria. Beth is a seamstress. Business has gone bad after having their son Joseph. They depend solely on Ben for all financial needs. Beth in turn keeps the home and serves her husband like a king.*

*Ben comes to the UK to do his master's degree and afterwards gets a job. He brings over his wife and son to the UK. After 2 years in the UK, finally, Beth can do some part-time work to get some money. This has created tension in the family. Ben wants her to use the money for family upkeep so that he can also save his salary for major projects at home.*

*When they came to see the counsellor, it was revealed that:*

*Ben's plan was to keep his money to build two houses, one for the couple and the other for his mum. However, Beth did not know about this plan because Ben did not discuss this with Beth. Ben also keeps all his financial statements, bank cards and internet banking login details away from Beth.*

*Beth also confessed that she is hiding some of her money from Ben because she does not trust him. She was however frustrated that even though Ben keeps his money, he wants her to give an account of every kobo she earns.*

*Ben said that, in their culture, it is unlawful for a wife to disrespect her husband by hiding her money. He says the husband is in charge of every estate of the family. Ben felt that bringing Beth to the UK has been a big mistake. This is because Beth always did as she was told when they were in Nigeria. But since she has been in the UK, she no longer obeys him.*

The case of Beth and Ben above is an example of the confusion that exists in many marriages, especially those who relocate to cities and abroad. How do couples reconcile their culture, traditions and values with their new residence?

It is a very common phenomenon which is blowing up many African marriages.

**CHECKPOINT**

What would be your advice for Ben and Beth to settle their financial differences?

How do you and your spouse manage your finances with respect to a situation such as this one?

CHAPTER FOUR

# Finding the Right Balance

*"But people who long to be rich fall into temptation and are trapped by many foolish and harmful desires that plunge them into ruin and destruction. For the love of money is the root of all kinds of evil. And some people, craving money, have wandered from the true faith and pierced themselves with many sorrows."*

1 TIMOTHY 6 :9-10 (NLT)

I hope all couples appreciate this: we marry to help each other fulfil our potential. Wives must do their bit to ease the pressure on husbands. Husbands with heavy financial pressure on them are unlikely to be funny, affectionate, loving and romantic.

Husbands must also help their wives to get the best out of their lives. Similarly, wives with financial and many household chore pressures will be unhappy, moody and tired.

Women have many responsibilities at home so husbands must be careful not to overburden them with financial pressures, if possible.

If for any reason the wife is the breadwinner or part of the workforce, it is only fair for the husband to make his wife feel loved and appreciated.

The husband should do all he can to support his wife physically, emotionally and even spiritually. Loving wives would not complain or rebel if they find the love and support of their husbands. It is a balancing act that must be done carefully with love. The more you give, the more you will receive from your partner. You scratch my back and I scratch yours even more gently. Love in action.

## BEING FAIR TO YOUR SPOUSE

Many married couples have a misunderstanding about how to handle their money. There are therefore inequalities and imbalances which divide husbands and wives. These misunderstandings have to do with appreciating that:

1. Both the husband and wife need money
2. Each one's money belongs to the family

### Understanding That the Husband and Wife Equally Need Money

Just as the wife needs money, in much the same way, the husband also needs money. One fundamental reason both men and women go to work is to make money. If your wife or husband followed you to a big city or abroad, it is because they believed you would get more money to improve your living conditions.

**CHECKPOINT**

Discuss how you can support each other's ambitions and dreams.

Understand that money is ultimately the number one reason men and women travel abroad. But how much are you prepared to sacrifice to get money?

Then the Bible through Apostle Paul gave this stern warning:

1 TIMOTHY 6:9-10 (NLT)
*"But people who long to be rich fall into temptation and are trapped by many foolish and harmful desires that plunge them into ruin and destruction. For the love of money is the root of all kinds of evil. And some people, craving money, have wandered from the true faith and pierced themselves with many sorrows."*

I hope all couples take this warning seriously and ensure that in your quest to improve your lives, you do not get trapped by the 'Love-of-Money syndrome'.

When people love money, they will do anything to get it. When people love money, they put a higher premium on money than human lives and relationships. In fact, when people love money, they will worship money instead of God. Such people may sell their bodies (prostitution), soul (conscience) and spirit (denying heaven) in search of money.

MATTHEW 16:26 (NLT)
*And what do you benefit if you gain the*
*whole world but lose your own soul?*
*Is anything worth more than your soul?"*

## Do Not Trade Your Marriage

Unfortunately, the devil has succeeded in buying peoples' bodies, souls and spirits in exchange for money. Such purchases ultimately include every property the family has— the children, your spirituality and your cherished marriage. Some husbands and wives are oblivious to the wiles of the enemy or Satan. They have given him access to take over their marriages whilst the couples focus on making money.

In the end, you may have money but you can lose your marriage. Such a couple may fight over every cent or penny. When they thought that money will make them happy, the same money became the number one source of their unhappiness and discontentment.

### *How couples throw away their marriages*

i. They would pick every extra shift at work. They are in a hurry to grab all Pounds, Dollars or Euros.

ii. They would avoid church and fellowship to make money. They think God can wait. Find excuses to tell elders and pastors.

iii. They would miss their children's school appointments. They show no interest in their children's education and activities. They do not help kids to do homework. If kids are struggling at school, they do not see. If children are playing truant, they do not see.

iv. They miss doctors' appointments. Doctors' appointments are a waste of time for them. They self-medicate and use any herbs or medicine recommended by friends.

v. They have no time for exercise and relaxation. They do not care too much about regular exercise. It is also a waste of time. They think it is probably a white man's routine. They feel strong and invincible. They have no time to rest because they feel they are losing money!

vi. They have no family time, they are a waste of time. It is one shift after another. There's no time for family devotion or prayers. If they pray at all, it is for a maximum of two minutes.

vii. They sleep very little. Of course, why should they sleep when they can make a few quid? They say sleep is for the weak.

viii. There's no time to further their education and update their skills. Time spent on further education would have made them a few pounds richer.
ix. There's no time for holidays. They would not waste money earned to go on holiday. They feel the holiday is a drain.
x. There's no time to meet up with friends. They lose touch with friends because they are too busy.

I understand that there comes a time when the couple has a pressing need for cash, and both may decide to sacrifice rest and comfort to make extra cash. But this should not become a routine to stretch the peace and stability of marriage.

Obviously, the desire for money at any cost will come back to hurt couples big time if they carry on like that for a long time.

## Do Not Be Breadcrumbed!

All the above is a trap. Please open your eyes. Money alone is not the real deal.

The devil is cunning. He dashes a few crumbs of bread, and most people just fall for it. One of the reasons why Europeans live longer is taking time off work to rest. They work very hard but when they complete their shifts at work, they do not chase overtime or extra shifts as most Africans do.

They increase the number of shifts only for a short time if they need money for a specific purpose. They have time for appointments and their kids. They exercise. They eat healthily. They go on holiday. And they rest. They have a good quality of life. If you want to live longer, enjoy your marriage and children. Do not fall for breadcrumbs.

### Each One's Money Belongs to the Family

You see, when my dad worked, his money belonged to him. In Western culture, your money belongs to the whole family.

If you need to fall on social benefits of any kind, your family income is assessed. If your children go to university, their maintenance grant is based on your family income. If you want to have a mortgage, the family income is assessed.

So, unless we accept this concept and appreciate the conditions and terms of your new environment and be open to each other, couples will struggle with their finances. So many couples from Africa living in the diaspora struggle because of a lack of understanding and cooperation with each other.

That brings us to the next chapter.

CHAPTER FIVE

# Financial Control and Abuse

There are many husbands and wives who are in abusive relationships but are unaware. If you try to control your partner's money, you might not be aware but it is possible you are abusing him or her.

Trying to control your spouse and their finances can leave them with fear, anxiety and uncertainty in the relationship. It is dangerous to instil fear into your spouse with the aim of controlling them and their finance.

Usually, when the ones being controlled finally get to know their rights in the country of residence, it is the beginning of troubles and sorrows in the marriage. Then the one controlling starts crying as a victim. What we tend to hear is: 'I brought this person to Europe, but he or she has really changed. This person has been influenced by bad friends and is hiding money.'

## WHERE DOES CONTROL COME FROM?

1. The one who earns higher feels he/she is entitled to have control over the other.
2. When the spouses who brought the partners overseas feel they brought them to make money for them.
3. When headship is taken to mean controlling the wife.
4. When a big bride price means owning the spouse.

Couples must guard against controls which can lead to abuse. Couples must work together as equals in the marriage.

### Case Study

*Sam 55 came to Germany at the age of 25. He left his long-term girlfriend with whom he had a son in Nigeria to seek greener pastures. After 15 long years, Sam returned to Abuja to formally marry his fiancée. Two years later, Alice got a visa to join her husband in Frankfurt. Alice did not work for a long time due to the language barrier. Sam did not allow her to go out without him. When she finally got a cleaning job after 5 years, all her money went into her husband's account because she had no bank account of her own. All child benefits went into Sam's bank account. Alice had to beg Sam for every cent to buy food or for personal use. The marriage is now over, after 15 years of living together in Frankfurt. What was wrong in this marriage?*

You see, when we don't re-adjust, things get out of hand.

1. Sam did not consider Alice as his equal because she had just come.
2. Sam felt Alice was not clever because she was a mere seamstress in Abuja without qualification.
3. Sam controlled Alice because a friend's wife 'rebelled' when she arrived from Gambia.
4. He never encouraged Alice to take German lessons to learn the language. He neither helped her integrate into society.
5. Sam spoke on her behalf on all appointments including attending doctors' appointments.
6. Sam never showed her where the church was, even though Alice was a Christian.
7. She was not allowed to have a friend.
8. She had no money of her own to send any remittances to her mum or family in Abuja.
9. She did not have enough money to make phone calls to them.
10. They had two children during the period but Alice never knew of anything called 'child benefit'.
11. She never wore any decent clothes or dresses because Sam bought everything for her.
12. When Alice worked all her wages went into Sam's bank account.
13. Sam dictated what she used her money for.

### How did Alice get out?

When her children started to go to school, Alice had to drop them off at school. It was here that she met another Nigerian lady and they started chatting all the time. Ola asked Alice intelligent questions when she realised she wore the same clothes every time.

Ola helped her register for German lessons and after one year, Alice was able to understand and write a few sentences. She could now read letters sent to their home. All this happened at the blindside of Sam. Alice after 2 years felt empowered and understood her rights living in Germany. She could now attend all appointments by herself. She could walk to the job centre to look for jobs. At long last she was free!

Sam was seething when he realised that Alice was now working, controlling her own money because she had her own bank account. Sam blamed Ola. He told all his friends that Ola had turned his wife against him. But the question is, who actually was in the wrong? Sam physically abused her and threatened to kill her.

## Don't Kill Each Other Because of Money

Issues with money in many African marriages abroad have led to serious conflicts, physical abuse, divorce and killings.

It is sad to state that as a couple and family counsellor, I have met couples who do not form a tight-knit family. Neither the husband nor the wife has left their mother and father to cleave to each other. Such couples have their eyes fixed on their family of origin. To such a couple, their family is where their mother, father and siblings are. They steal from the husband or wife to give to their parents and siblings. They behave as if to say, this marriage is only a transit. It is just a matter of time and they are out. In the back of their minds, they have already concluded that this marriage will not work. When couples have such a mentality, they do not try to solve any problem in the marriage.

Make your spouse, children and marriage your priority. In the sight of God, this is your responsibility. You will account to God the way you looked after your marriage. You vowed to wed with all your earthly goods, why are you hiding your money?

Remitting big sums of money to your families and friends that aren't from your country of origin and neglecting the welfare of your spouse and children is a form of abuse.

CHECKPOINT

**Ladies and gentlemen:**

How much pressure do you both face from your families back home when it comes to giving financial support?

How has travelling abroad affected the way you handle money in your marriage?

CHAPTER SIX

# Avoiding Financial Infidelity

*"One who is faithful in a very little is also faithful in much, and one who is dishonest in a very little is also dishonest in much. If then you have not been faithful in the unrighteous wealth, who will entrust to you the true riches? And if you have not been faithful in that which is another's, who will give you that which is your own"?*

LUKE 16:10-12 (ESV)

*"Don't love money;*
*be satisfied with what you have.*
*For God has said, "I will never fail you.*
*I will never abandon you."*

HEBREW 13:5 (NLT)

## REFLECTION

- **Gentlemen:**

    1. As head of the family, how much do you earn and how much do you spend on major bills at home?
    2. How much of your financial spending does your wife know about?
    3. Are you willing to let your wife know about all your bank passwords, Pins and go through your bank statements?
    4. How easy have you made it for your wife to discuss financial matters with you?

- **Ladies:**

    1. As a helper to the man and the family, how much do you earn and what percentage of your income goes to support your husband and the family?
    2. Does your husband know all your income and your expenditure?
    3. Do you discuss how much you want to spend or remit abroad?
    4. How easy do you find it to share your finances with your husband?

## FINANCIAL INFIDELITY IN AFRICAN MARRIAGES

As a family and couples' counsellor, one of the most sensitive issues I have to deal with in marriages is couples' finances. This is usually about the abuse of the couple's income, unauthorised spending, hiding savings and unpaid bills. These have led to suspicion, loss of trust, arguments and separation.

Financial infidelity is when couples lie about their finances. It is possible for just one person or both to do that. It is probably the number one problem that affects many marriages, even among Christian families.

The bitter truth is that many African couples are not honest with money in their marriages due to history, culture and huge expectations from their families of origin.

Keeping financial secrets is very common in many African marriages because many people do not fully leave families to cleave to their spouses. There is a family behind our family. Couples need to talk and agree on how to use the family money on anything, including remittances.

If couples can master the skill of transparency, honesty and fairness, they will have a great marriage. However, if they take their partners for granted in this important area, their marriage will be as good as dead.

O, how I wish there was a school dedicated to training couples or would-be couples on how to correctly manage money in their marriages. If there were a one-size-fits-all approach, how helpful that would be! But whether you know how to manage money or not, the basic principle is simple: you have a duty to be fair to your spouse. Cheating and hiding money from your spouse is the beginning of the end of your marriage.

**Case Study of Elder Joe and Deaconess Joanna**

*A case was brought to my pastor friend of a couple who are both officers of the church, Elder Joe and a Deaconess Joanna. They were at each other's throats over a sum of money. Elder Joe was demanding an amount of £15,000 from his wife which was the cost he paid to bring her from Ghana to the UK.*

*But Deaconess Joanna insisted she wouldn't pay a dime because she had been serving her husband faithfully. She cooked for him, gave him good sex and other fringe benefits as a wife. Elder Joe was mad at her because she was building a house in Ghana while they still rented in the UK. Besides, that was not discussed with him and he only heard about it from an external source. Deaconness Joanna insisted her mum's condition in Ghana required an urgent need for a house. She claimed if she had told her husband, he would never have agreed for her to provide accommodation for her sick mum.*

You are probably thinking how could Elder Joe demand money from his own wife?

When the couple appeared before their pastor, the following were uncovered:

- The couple had separate bank accounts.
- Elder Joe paid for all rent and bills in the house.
- Deaconess Joanna paid for food and their children's stuff.

- Deaconess Joanna had the children's benefits coming into her bank account.
- Deaconess Joanna determined what Elder Joe ate for dinner because she bought the foodstuff.
- Elder Joe is still paying for loans he took to get Deaconess Joanna to the UK.
- The Couple was separated from each other for 10 years before Deaconess Joanna joined him in the UK.
- They were both suspicious of the actual money each earned.
- Elder Joe had no house in Ghana even though he had been in Europe for ten years.
- Elder Joe was sending all money earned to his wife to support the family and build a house for them.
- Deaconess Joanna felt obliged to provide accommodation for her mum as a 'thank you' gesture.
- Deaconess Joanna felt her money was hers after paying for food and sorting out the children.
- Elder Joe was keeping two jobs to be able to pay for rent and bills.
- Elder Joe wanted to work hard to keep the marriage but did not feel the support of his wife.
- He felt that if his wife helped him pay off the loan, they would be okay.
- The couple hardly had time to do anything together.
- The couple said they felt they were living under one roof as housemates and not as husband and wife.

- Elder Joe felt he had wasted his money bringing over his wife and children to the UK.
- Joanna seemed not bothered if the marriage was dissolved because it might afford her the chance to get a council house.

### WHY COUPLES LIE ABOUT THEIR FINANCES

Among many things, the main things that cause couples to lie about their finances are:

- Yielding to pressure from family and friends back in Africa.
- Fear of disagreeing with spouse may result in conflict.
- If a spouse thinks he/she brings more money home.

### AREAS OF FINANCIAL INFIDELITY

Most financial disagreements are centred on the following:

1. Hiding the payslips/cheques and bank statements
2. Failing to disclose all the income
3. Secret spending and remittances
4. Pretending not to have money
5. Undertaking secret projects

You must make a conscious effort to be fair to your spouse. Be determined not to be that *Cheat* in your own home.

To be able to do that, there are a few questions that you have to ask yourself:

## Are You Under Financial Pressure?

1. What prevents you from being honest and transparent in your marriage?
2. Are you under any pressure from your family of origin or someone else to steal from your own home? You see, this is your home. If you steal from here, you are stealing from yourself. Besides, if you love your spouse, I am sure you would want to have the very best of marriage with them.
3. Are You Just Being Dishonest?
4. Where did you learn to be dishonest with money in your marriage? Some people believe that those who cheat on finances are more likely to cheat in other areas. So if you are lying to your spouse about your finances, is it something you learned from your society? Or is it that you cheat about everything and not just on money? If you don't want to be called a cheat and dishonest person, what are you going to do about this before you are found out?
5. Are you struggling to control your infidelity? You might have seen how this affected your parents', friends' or your own marriage? There is always help out there if you are willing to seek help. Your friend, your pastor, your counsellor and even your spouse can be your first point of call. But you must first admit that you need help.

6. Are you fair to your spouse? Do you treat him or her the way you want to be treated? It is always said, to treat others how you want to be treated. What is your reaction if someone is not honest with you? Do you get angry and play the victim if you uncover anything your spouse hides from you? You can make this marriage work by treating that gift God has given you with respect and fairness.

CHAPTER SEVEN

# Resolving Financial Infidelity

*"I, (name), do take you, (name) to be my lawful wedded wife/husband, to have and to hold from this day forward; for better, for worse, for richer, for poorer, in sickness and in health, to love and to cherish, till death us do us part, according to God's holy law. In the presence of God I make this vow."*

Because financial nakedness cuts deep into the heart of any relationship, finding a solution can be challenging. It requires identifying the core of any disagreement, willingness of the couple to forgive their spouse, and initiating strategies to prevent its occurrence. Married couples must always remember the vow they made to each other in the presence of God to be faithful to each other during their marriage ceremony.

## THINGS COUPLES MOSTLY DISAGREE ON IN RELATION TO THEIR FINANCES

- **Joint Bank Account or Separate Bank Accounts**

  If for any reason you cannot have a joint account, then couples should be very clear on what each will contribute to the family pot. How do you save the spare money?

- **How Much Money to Spend on Each Other's Family**

  Everyone's family expects remittance. Couples should agree on the amount to be remitted each month.

- **Where to Build the Family House in Africa**

  Do we build at the wife's or husband's home? Agree on which location best fits you as a couple. The couple may consider cultural values too.

- **Where is Our Home, Europe or Africa?**

  Ensure you secure where you live first before you think about your country of origin unless you are relocating in the next couple of years.

- **Bills and Renting**

  Who should pay what? If a couple has a joint account, all rents/mortgage, bills and other expenditures are paid from there. It makes life easier. The remainder, after all deductions can go into the savings pot after shopping for yourselves and the home.

### Who Keeps the Children's Benefits and Tax Credits?

It is not adult benefits. It is for children's upkeep. It is expected that no one touches this unless it is going to buy stuff for the kids.

**WAYS COUPLES CAN SAVE THEMSELVES FINANCIAL INFIDELITY STRUGGLES**

- Declare to each other your commitment to making this marriage work.
- Understand that your family is your husband/wife and children.
- Identify and agree to financial commitment in Africa, especially remittance to parents.
- Agree on how much, based on your current income, you can part away with each month.
- Agree on what you both consider an emergency that requires urgent action.
- Decide if you want to have a joint account and be faithful to it. Again if you agree to have separate bank accounts, be honest and transparent with each other about your income and expenditures.
- Based on your spending patterns, agree on who should be in charge of the finances if you have a joint account.
- If separate accounts, decide how the rent/mortgage, bills and food should be paid. Couples must be flexible and open because your financial source can change and you will need your partner to support you.

- Develop a savings habit for the family now.
- Learn to live within your means.
- Discuss your payslips/paycheques from time to time and appraise each other especially if they have earned more than usual.
- Make your Bank statements available to your spouse if required without feeling upset. It will make your partner have more confidence in you and your spending.
- Disclose and share your internet or online banking login details with each other. It is also important to make known the Pin for your credit and debit cards.
- Create capacity to talk about how to increase your income and how to reduce expenditure.
- Communicate with each other your dependants apart from your children and how you are going to support them.
- Agree with your partner about your financial goals and how to achieve them.
- Talk about your dreams. Your dream jobs, cars, houses, etc. Discuss how you can help each other to achieve those dreams.

There is usually one complaint about the couples' income: that couples are hiding their wages from each other or one person is hiding his/her income. In Europe, couples' income stays almost the same if they are doing the same hours so it should not be difficult for couples to know how much each person is paid.

## WHEN THERE IS FINANCIAL INFIDELITY IN YOUR MARRIAGE

1. It is time to talk frankly. If you suspect your partner is cheating on your finances, you must have your concerns, anger, sense of betrayal, and helplessness and hurt voiced out.
2. If you are the one cheating, you have to admit you made a mistake. Make a decision to be honest, open, and keep your promises. Accept your responsibility for bringing financial infidelity into your marriage. We all make mistakes. No point trying to defend the indefensible. Just accept your mistakes and apologise.
3. Discuss how this happened and how this can be avoided. There should be room to be open and transparent with each other if you want to have a successful marriage.

- Follow this up with a weekly or monthly discussion. Show interest but do not try to be an angel. Make time to check on your accounts together and talk about upcoming bills, issues, goals, hopes and dreams.
- Try to spend monies together. Improve your togetherness by eating out, going on holiday or visiting places.

## COUPLES' ACTIVITIES

### Financial Openness Challenge

| Activity | Husband | Wife |
|---|---|---|
| *What motivates you to work hard for money?* | | |
| *How many jobs and hours do you work?* | | |
| *How much do you have in your savings accounts?* | | |
| *How many credit cards do you have?* | | |
| *What are your online bank details?* | | |
| *What are your PINS for your debit and credit cards?* | | |
| *How easy it is for you to be open with your finances?* | | |

## Conclusion

Money has gained so much attention in the world. Our understanding of our past, culture and religion and how they have shaped us will help us appreciate our partners' points of view when it comes to managing our finances.

African marriages in the diaspora are affected by many unsuspecting factors. Usually, couples who have just immigrated have no clue what is affecting their marriage. If couples can rise above these challenges to develop a workable and amicable strategy, they will have the best marriage.

Some couples have loved money and have entered marriages because of it. In the end, the same money has caused them pain, distress, shame and even death. Beware that you do not pierce yourself with the knife called 'Love-of-money'. Money is good for marriage but when it is mishandled, it can be a very bad master. Be open, fair and transparent with your spouse and you will have a peaceful and enjoyable marriage irrespective of your financial situation. Wishing you a satisfying and transparent financial life in your marriage.

PART

# 4

# SEX AND ROMANCE IN MARRIAGE

*Sex is* NOT *just an act of penetration,*
*it is the communion and the pleasure*
*of the body, soul and spirit.*

*Sex is intimacy and fellowship.*
*But when couples have unresolved issues,*
*this intimacy is lost and sex*
*becomes a boring chore.*

CHAPTER ONE

# Sex: God's Free Gift for Married Couples

This part of the book is not about how to have sex. Rather, it addresses reasons couples may stay away from having sex. It is about understanding that sex is good for both the man and the woman. So, couples should gather all efforts and resources to make sex happen regularly. Also, sex life is greatly improved when the couples are honest and genuine about how they feel about intercourse.

Sex is one of the greatest gifts God gave to mankind. It is free, it is always present and it is absolutely pleasurable. The benefits to both the man and woman are endless as we will find out later. These benefits are well documented or projected in magazines, books, radio, social media and even in the Bible. It is one of the most beautiful and intimate activities in the marital life of a couple.

Sex can be seen as your acceptance of one's love and commitment in a relationship. A marital relationship where sex has not taken place is usually considered not consummated. This is because sex is considered the seal of marriage. It is also considered the glue that binds married couples together.

## REVIEWING OUR SEX LIFE AS A COUPLE

Unfortunately, sex is one thing that is least talked about in the open among Christian couples, the family, the church and society at large. Certain cultures even forbid the mentioning of vagina or penis because it is considered a taboo talking about private parts. When couples have issues in their relationship that have to do with sex, they are mostly unable to discuss them because they are considered private issues. Church leaders even shy away from such issues relating to sex as though it were disgusting, evil and unholy. Young couples are left on their own and they have no place to turn to for help.

Many marriages are suffering from what I refer to as 'sex anaemia'. In my seminars, only two out of ten couples rate sex as satisfactory, and one out of ten as good. These figures do not relate to the quality of the sexual activity alone but the number of times couples engage in it as well. This is because couples do not prioritise their sex life and ultimately fail to make time for each other. No wonder many married men and women are involved in extra-marital affairs. It is time to put an end to us suffering in silence. It is about time couples open up and become honest about sex. It is time to talk about it, discuss it and find ways of improving and enjoying it.

## BREAKING THE TABOO

Ann Summers recently launched the Pleasure Positivity Project. This research was to gain insight into how couples are communicating about sex, and the results revealed that only two in five (42%) women felt fully satisfied after sex with their partner, compared to 52% of men. When it came to communication in the bedroom, 59% of Brits said they felt comfortable discussing their sexual desires with their partner and 40% discussed their sex life with their partner on a weekly basis. Despite this, 20% of British women said they were not comfortable discussing any sexual subjects with their partner (Ann Summers Positive Pleasure Project research, 2019).

The statistics above clearly show that even in western cultures where sex and sexuality are quite liberal, many people still feel very uncomfortable discussing sex in their relationships.

In certain African and Asian cultures where discussing sex is considered a taboo or sacred, couples sometimes feel they would be judged for discussing issues having to do with sex. If 50% of couples in a sexual relationship are not satisfied and yet do not communicate this to their partners, this could only be a set-up for disaster. Couples should be open and honest about sex, whether satisfied or not, needing more or less.

### How Frequently Do We Have Sex?

British National Survey of Sexual attitudes and lifestyles in the UK reported the following shocking statistics among UK couples according to age brackets:

- 16–44-year olds: less than 50% have sex at least once a week.
- 35–44-year olds: females two times per month; males three times per month
- Typically couples under 30 years: on the average twice a week.
- 40–50-year olds: less than once a week.
- 50–60-year olds: twice a month.

(Wellings et al, 2019)

These numbers are very concerning considering that sex is free among married couples and has great benefits for the couple. These numbers tell that there is definitely something affecting couples' sexual drives.

> *Simon said, "My appetite for sex has disappeared since we migrated to Norway. The cold plays a big part but the pressure to get our immigration status sorted gives me no desire for sex."*
>
> *Simon wasn't alone, his wife Maria had this to say, "The last time I really enjoyed sex with Simon is about two years ago. His reaction to my complaints about our sex life leaves me feeling judged and condemned. I do not only love sex; I enjoy cuddling but it seems what we do in bed is only on Simon's terms. I only have to hope and pray he comes round to me."*

## MARRIED LIFE IS A CRUCIBLE

A crucible is a ceramic or metal container in which metals or other substances may be melted or subjected to very high temperatures. Marriage and love are a crucible. There are many interactive forces that come together to create a good marriage and a good sexual life. To have sex or not, is not as simple as you might think. There are many things that go on in your life that take your mind off sex or enhance your sexual desire.

To some couples, sex is too much hard work. And to others, they just can't be bothered. It is the same routine, in the same place and lacks innovation, creativity and style. Let's look at some of the forces that affect a couple's disposition to sex at a particular point in time.

### The State of Your Inner Man

How you feel at a particular time definitely affects your sex drive. Are you feeling excited or do you like the things around you? When it is so, it will be easy for you to feel horny. The reverse is also true. When you are feeling low, stressed, depressed and annoyed, sex is a secondary issue.

For instance, if the people around you are annoying you—your spouse, your children, your in-laws, your friends and even your work colleagues or clients—it affects your sex drive negatively.

**Your Pressures**

Pressures such as financial demands from home, bills to pay, daily traffic, childcare and other such obligations take couples' minds off sex.

All these interactions and many more play on our minds all the time whether we admit them or not. Understand that not all spouses can spot your stresses and pressures until you clearly tell them. You need to voice it out. Some ladies and gentlemen are very emotionally intelligent and they can pick cues easily from their partners and help them out. If you are not married to someone like that, then you need to inform them about what you may be going through emotionally.

**CHECKPOINT**

Discuss with your spouse if he or she is happy with your sex life. If they are not, find out why?

How comfortable are you, discussing sex with your spouse?

CHAPTER TWO

# Six Great Mysteries Behind Sex

*When you have sex with me, it is not just sex;*
*it is my world, my chambers and*
*my vulnerability that you just entered.*

*And Adam knew Eve his wife;*
*and she conceived, and bare Cain, and said,*
*I have gotten a man from the LORD.*

GENESIS 4:1 (KJV)

Having sexual intimacy with your spouse is one of the greatest gifts that couples enjoy. Whether you are hugging, caressing, snuggling or having penetrative sex, all these come with great benefits. It is a secret and a mystery that most couples are not aware of; hence, they take sex for granted.

In this section, you will discover six mysteries and secrets that would motivate you to strive to initiate and enjoy the act of sex as couple.

Let us investigate the six greatest mysteries about sex:

1. It provides deeper knowledge of spouses
2. It glues couple so they become one
3. It deepens sweet fellowship
4. It is the power for procreation
5. It quenches sexual lust
6. It is a source of good health and vitality

GENESIS 4:1

*And Adam knew Eve his wife; and she conceived, and bare Cain, and said, I have gotten a man from the LORD (KJV)*

*Now Adam had sexual relations with his wife, Eve, and she became pregnant. When she gave birth to Cain, she said, "With the LORD's help, I have produced a man!" (NLT)*

## 1. PROVISION OF DEEPER KNOWLEDGE OF YOUR SPOUSE

Do you want to learn and know your spouse intimately and deeply? One of the greatest ways to do that is to have regular sex. People in love relationships usually open up and bare it all in lovemaking.

There is no greater way of knowing someone more intimately than having sex with that person. It is the greatest height you can ascent to know someone, whether they are your spouse or not.

"Adam knew his wife..." The Hebrew word for "knew" is "Yadah" which is translated in English as follows:

- To learn
- Find out
- Know by experience
- To know
- Recognise the nature and uses of someone

The mystery here is that when you have sex, you are learning intimately about your partner; their actions and behaviours. You are also finding out what they are and what they are not. It helps you see some things about them that neither their parents, siblings, friends nor bodyguards know and will ever know. This is an extremely deep knowledge.

Do you remember when the Queen of Sheba came to see Solomon? She observed in some things in his chambers.

Listen to her,

> *She said to the king, "The report I heard in my own country about your achievements and your wisdom is true. But I did not believe these things until I came and saw with my own eyes. Indeed, not even half was told me; in wisdom and wealth you have far exceeded the report I heard.*
>
> I KINGS 6:6-7 (NIV)

The Bible does not explicitly reveal how far the queen went into the chambers of King Solomon. But her expression may mean the king took her into deep places. The queen saw many remarkable things herself.

So, when you are with your lover in their chambers, in their privacy, you get a revelation of exactly who and what they are in their manners, attitude and possessions. You have a first-hand experience of them. Before you get into their chambers, you may have many assumptions and expectations about them. Love and love making gives you the experience.

The same expression was used by Paul, who, in spite of his wealth of experience, still wanted to know Christ. He wanted to be in God's presence over and over again. He wanted to learn, know, and experience Christ more intimately. This is how he expressed his desire:

> *"That I may know Him, and the power of His resurrection, and the fellowship of His sufferings, being made conformable unto His death…"*
>
> PHIL 3:10 (NIV)

### Dora and Des

> *Dora said, "I knew Des when we were 15 years old in college. I thought I knew him, but I was wrong. I knew him properly after we married 10 years later. I have learnt a lot about him. I have also experienced what love really is".*

In knowledge there is intelligence. Sex is a terrific way of gaining intelligence. Having sex with your partner gives you that advantage. Do you understand why in movies, spies usually use beautiful ladies to trap men or to gain information and intelligence?

Do you remember how Samson was trapped by Delilah? When she slept with him, he revealed all the information and secrets he was not supposed to share. This caused his downfall. Let us see how Delilah got the information from Samson to the Philistines.

### Samson and Delilah

> *And when Delilah saw that he had told her all his heart, she sent and called for the lords of the Philistines, saying, Come up this once, for he hath shewed me all his heart. Then the lords of the Philistines came up unto her, and brought money in their hand. And she made him sleep upon her knees; and she called for a man, and she caused him to shave off the seven locks of his head; and she began to afflict him, and his strength went from him.*
>
> JUDGES 16:18-19 (KJV)

There are intruders who want to use sexual powers to trap you and your spouse. Both of you have a duty to satisfy each other sexually. If you don't, you are in danger of being exposed to the outside world once your partner starts sleeping around. It might not be intentional but there is a huge risk of revealing family plans, secrets and promises of God for your family.

### Jack and Jill

*Jill narrated her story to the counsellor, "I know Jack and we have not been of ourselves for the past year. Our 2-year-old son has a condition we have never told anyone about, apart from the doctors. I want Jack to tell me if he is not having anything to do Eva, the lady I once suspected he was having an affair with. She met me at the shopping mall, and she was asking me about our sick child and how we are preparing for our summer holiday in Maldives. These are things we do not even tell our family members."*

*This was Jack's response, "I feel so ashamed to have slept with this woman. I slept with her but she had no right to confront my wife and disclose any conversation we had. I have learnt my lessons in a hard way. I can only say I am sorry."*

It is common knowledge that couples who have too many things on their minds are less likely to be interested in sex. But couples should work hard to be intimate again as soon as possible to prevent infidelity and its undesirable effects.

## 2. BECOMING ONE WITH YOUR SPOUSE

*"And said, 'For this reason a man will leave his father and mother and be united to his wife, and the two will become one flesh.'"*

MATTHEW 19:5 (NIV)

> *"Do you not know that your bodies are members of Christ himself? Shall I then take the members of Christ and unite them with a prostitute? Never! Do you not know that he who unites himself with a prostitute is one with her in body? For it is said, "The two will become one flesh." But whoever is united with the Lord is one with Him in spirit."*
>
> **1 CORINTHIANS 6:15-17**

One of the most beautiful things to observe among couples is oneness. When couples are united, it reflects on them and their family. It creates calmness and stability in the marriage. When couples are not united, you can see chaos, discontentment, and disagreement between them. Sex with your partner offers that unity, calmness, and contentment.

Three things happen in sexual unity:

- Bonding
- Becoming One flesh
- Yoking together

There are three persons in godly and Christian marriages. These are husband, wife and God. Three is stability, two is not. Couples are united with Christ.

When you are married and have sex, it has godly approval. It is holy. It is binding and it is unifying! Sad news is that due to its binding power, whoever you have sex with becomes attached to this relationship. They have interest and estates in the marriage. Sex has power. Sex is not just sex. It is a glue that binds people together. If you do not mean it, please have no sex with people you have no idea about.

### You are Becoming One Flesh

You have only one flesh and that is for your husband or wife. It is one plus one equals one. Mathematically, 1+1=1. It is not 1+2=1.

Any unknown quantity in the equation destabilises the equilibrium. It is only in marriage that this equation is applicable. No one fully understands it, but you must accept it. It is a mystery. It is more spiritual than meets the eye. We are members of Christ's body. See how Apostle Paul explained it:

> *"In this same way, husbands ought to*
> *love their wives as their own bodies.*
> *He who loves his wife loves himself.*
> *After all, no one ever hated their own body,*
> *but they feed and care for their body,*
> *just as Christ does the church—*
> *for we are members of His body."*
>
> EPHESIANS 5:28-30 (NIV)

From the Scripture above, we can deduce some secrets about what the husband's roles are in helping the couple to become one body:

1. Through the husband's love for the wife.
2. When husband loves the wife the same way he loves his own body.

3. When husbands clothe and feed their wives just as he does to his own body.
4. When the husband emulates what Christ does for the church.
5. When the husband acts as the head over the wife and family.
6. Christ died for the church so should the husband. Christ got His life back, so will the husband. But just as Christ did not seek His own, so should husbands not seek their own.

## Yoking Together

> *Do not be yoked together with unbelievers. For what do righteousness and wickedness have in common? Or what fellowship can light have with darkness.*
>
> 2 Corinthians 6:14 (NIV)

This Scripture is usually used by Christians in a negative sense to warn themselves against marrying or sleeping with unbelievers.

But if you flip the text over, it also admonishes couples to be yoked together. It admonishes them to be equally yoked with the righteous, and to be equally yoked with your wife as a husband. One of the strongest ways, as the Bible indicated above, to be yoked together is to have intimacy. Couples must appreciate this mystery and enjoy this intimacy.

The Bible does not say it but we all know that the more sex you have with your partner, the closer you become. Your love grows. You yearn for each other. You desire them to be around you. You tend to agree on even more things.

Naked couples should not miss this. It is not the prayer of the pastor that binds you together. It is the consummation of the marriage through sex.

When couples are naked, they are united physically, emotionally, and spiritually. They are united in fun times and tough times. That unity even speeds up prayer responses from God. Let's hear from our Lord Jesus Christ, His take on unity and prayer.

> *"Again, truly I tell you that if two of you on earth agree about anything they ask for, it will be done for them by my Father in heaven. For where two or three gather in my name, there am I with them."*
>
> MATTHEW 18:19-20 (NIV)

### Pearl and Seth

> *"When we haven't had sex for a long time, we also do not have appetite for prayer. I actually get angry when Seth hasn't touched me for days and wants us to pray. I get excited for prayer with Seth when our sex life is great. I may be selfish, but I cannot help it," Pearl noted.*
>
> *"I feel very moody and erratic if we go a few weeks without sex. I feel I am disconnected from Pearl.*

*Not only that, but spiritually, I lose fervour and desire," Seth said .*

Couples who are naked spend time and make effort to have more sex to strengthen the cord of love between them.

**CHECKPOINT**

What have you discovered about your spouse during love making?

Discuss with your spouse how lack of sex affects you and your marriage.

### 3. SWEET FELLOWSHIP

*"Do you not know that your bodies are members of Christ himself? Shall I then take the members of Christ and unite them with a prostitute? Never! Do you not know that he who unites himself with a prostitute is one with her in body? For it is said,*

*"The two will become one flesh." But whoever is united with the Lord is one with Him in spirit"*
1 CORINTHIANS 6:15-17 (NIV)

*"Do not be yoked together with unbelievers. For what do righteousness and wickedness have in common? Or what fellowship can light have with darkness?"* 2 CORINTHIANS 6:14 (NIV)

This is another great mystery. The Bible compares the relationship between husband and wife to Christ and the church. This is beautiful.

Great couples do not only have oneness and good intelligence about each other; they also have sweet fellowship with each other. They are equal fellows in the same ship, 'fellowship'. They have communion together and they consider each other as equal partners. They depend on each other. This is possible only if couple are both light! Light and darkness have no fellowship!

You can see that Apostle Paul is connecting fellowshipping with God with sex; physical connection with spiritual connection. This clearly demonstrates that the act of sex is not only physical, but truly spiritual as well.

Just as you worship God, you extend that worship to your spouse in lovemaking. Sex is therefore a deep spiritual connection with your spouse. When you are flooding each other with kindness, adulation and appreciation, they lead to emotional and spiritual connection. It is the only intimacy that is likened to the worship of God. No wonder couples lose spark and connectivity to God when their sexual life takes a nosedive. Just as you get united with Christ through fellowship, you do so in marriage through sexual intimacy. It is the reason you should not be yoked with someone who is a prostitute or not your spouse.

> *Do not be yoked together with unbelievers. For what do righteousness and wickedness have in common? Or what fellowship can light have with darkness?* 2 CORINTHIANS 6:14 (NIV)

You should therefore only have fellowship with your spouse and none with anyone else.

## 4. POWER FOR PROCREATION

> *Now Adam had sexual relations with his wife, Eve, and she became pregnant. When she gave birth to Cain, she said, "With the LORD's help, I have produced a man!"* (NLT)

Many women tell me their major reason for getting married is to have the chance to give birth to their own children.

You see, the most powerful men on earth, except Jesus, were not born by supernatural powers or mighty people; neither were they commanded from heaven. In fact, we are all products of ordinary men and women who had sex. They might not have planned our birth. They may not have been married. We may not have been born out of love; yet, we came out of them. It is simple: no sex, no man, and no propagation of the human race!

### Vivian and Jeff

*Vivian said this about having babies, "My main reason for getting married was to have children. I could not do it on my own. I love my husband, but I absolutely adore my children. I have three children, but I am looking for more. I know Jeff is not keen, but he will do it before he realises that I am pregnant. I know how to get him when I need my babies."*

*Jeff said, "I do not hate babies, but I wanted only two. When Vivian is all over me, I know what she wants anyway. She will flirt, kiss, and even cook my best and favourite dinner. She thinks I do not know her thoughts, but I do. It is only that at such times, she is simply irresistible."*

You might be the conduit of the gift to the world. Your act of love towards each other through sexual intercourse may give the world a mighty person that will transform lives. The engineers, astromists, physicists, doctors, nurses, politicians, humanitarians, etc., are all products of a man and a woman who had sex. Next time you are having sex, as pleasurable as it is, your act may result in the birth of a king, a president, prime minister, or any powerful person. It is, therefore, not just sex; it is the pathway to creating new human beings to populate the earth.

**CHECKPOINT**

How important is having children to you as a couple? Discuss how your marriage is or would be because of the children God has blessed you with.

## 5. QUENCHING THE FLAME OF LUST

*But if they can't control themselves,*
*they should go ahead and marry.*
*It's better to marry than to burn with lust.*

1 CORINTHIANS 7:9 (NLT)

Human beings are also sexual beings. Both men and women need sex.

No wonder God created Eve for Adam. Both men and women burn with passion or lust if they go a long time without sex.

Apostle Paul with all his spirituality acknowledged that without sex, most couples will fall into sexual temptation.

Prayer is not the answer. Bible study is not the answer. Married couples have the responsibility to satisfy each other with sex and more sex.

If you deny your spouse sex and they fall into sexual temptation, you will have to answer to God.

### 6. SOURCE OF GOOD HEALTH AND VITALITY

The importance of sex to our health is well documented. Scientists, psychologists, and experts believe that having regular sex boosts your immune system, reduces high blood pressure, slows down ageing, reduces stress and prolongs life.

#### Sam and Abi

> *"Last year, when Sam was working abroad and I was by myself, it was the most difficult period in our marriage so far. I could neither eat nor sleep well. I was visiting the hospital every month. All investigations by doctors proved nothing. This year, since Sam came back and started working from home, I have not visited the doctors in the last eight months. I am eating well. I sleep well, especially after intimacy," Abi narrated.*

It is proven that couples who stay together sleep better than those who are apart. They can connect well as well. The health benefits of sex are too many to be ignored in your marriage.

***Couples who are not having sex are denying themselves of what every human being desires and prays for—good health!***

The Bible does not outline the health benefits of good sex, but experts have done a great deal of work about it.

Studies have shown that sex is extremely beneficial to our health. Sex activates a variety of neurotransmitters that impact not only our brains, but also many other organs in our bodies. Sex helps to:

- **Lower Your Blood Pressure**

This is the bit that gets me excited. Lovemaking helps lower your blood pressure. Mail Online reported research conducted by Georgia State University, **"The more pleasurable the orgasm, the lower the blood pressure readings a day after intercourse."**

**Scientists found that volunteers' readings fell by up to 13% the day after making love. This result is similar to taking a water pill diuretic, a common treatment for high pressure.**

This, to me, is a no brainer. Pleasure and cure! And we know that the blood pressure medicines have side effects whereas the risk of having sex is very minimal, if any.

- **Lower Your Risk of Heart Attack**

Heart attacks kill too many people in the United Kingdom. According to the British Heart Foundation, it was the leading cause of death worldwide in 2019. In the UK, one in eight men and one in 14 women die from coronary heart disease. So, you see, if having sex will reduce the risk, you need to prioritise this in your routines. A good sex life is good for your heart. This is because sex counts as an exercise. No wonder it reduces your chances of heart attack. Pinzone of WebMD says, "Sex won't replace the treadmill, but it counts for something. It uses about five calories per minute, four more calories than watching TV. It gives you a one-two punch: it pumps up your heart rate and uses various muscles." Besides being a great way to raise your heart rate, sex helps keep your oestrogen and testosterone levels balanced.

## More Sex, Better Sleep

After a hard day's work, you want to retire to your bed with your spouse and have an amazing sleep. Sex, just like having good exercise, improves your sleep tremendously. Experts believe that sex alone does not make you sleepy, but the chemicals that are released during sex may help you sleep better. They believe sex works by boosting the 'cuddle' hormone oxytocin which helps reduce stress.

Other hormones, such as dopamine, prolactin, and progesterone, have all been implicated in affecting the mind with a sense of relief, relaxation, and sleepiness, following the act of satisfactory sex. Ladies and gentlemen, why toss and turn and struggle for sleep when your sleeping pill lies just next to you?

## Pam and Tony

> *"Since Tony took this new role as a marketing executive, he does not come to bed until midnight. I go to bed at 10.00pm. Sadly, we have not had sex in the past eight weeks. This has badly affected my sleep. He knows that my sleeping pill is when he cuddles me in bed or has sex with me. I feel like I am losing not just my best friend, but also my sleep," Pam said.*

### Better Immune System

This is another interesting one. Having regular sex improves your defences against colds and flu.

Scientists believe that people who have frequent sex (one to two times a week) have more immunoglobulin A (IgA) in their saliva. People who have infrequent sex (less than once a week) have significantly less IgA.

IgA is the antibody that plays a role in preventing illnesses and it is the first line of defence against human papillomavirus, or HPV.

These benefits of sex are so profound that, married couples need to do whatever it takes to improve their sex life.

That means, if your spouse is visiting the doctors all the time or taking cold medications, you might not be doing so well. The solution lies with you.

### LITTLE SECRET FOR THE MEN

I know that when it comes to having sexual intercourse, most men do not need a second invitation. But the following secrets may add more fire to your appetite:

**A recent review found that men who had more frequent penile-vaginal intercourse had less risk of developing prostate cancer.** One study found that men who averaged having 4.6 to 7 ejaculations a week were 36 percent less likely to receive a prostate cancer diagnosis before the age of 70. This is in comparison to men who reported ejaculating 2.3 or fewer times a week on average.

Lorelei Mucci, a co-author of the study and director of the Cancer Epidemiology and Cancer Prevention Program at the Harvard T.H. Chan School of Public Health says, "One potential explanation is the so-called prostate stagnation hypothesis: that infrequent ejaculation may allow potentially cancer-causing substances to linger in the prostate for extended periods of time, upping cancer risk."

Gentlemen, if this does not motivate you to raise the bar for sex, I am not sure what else would. There is a win-win situation for men.

## LITTLE SECRET FOR THE WOMEN

It is no secret that when women reach certain age group or bracket, sex becomes daunting for many of them. But the following revelations prove that sex is better for your body in your mid to the latter years of your life.

- It improves bladder control: Bladders can be weakened without sex. Sex serves as a muscle tightening agent and prevents many visits to the toilet per hour. This also means it can improve your incontinence.
- Increases vaginal lubrication: The more you abstain from sex, the drier you become. When you are dry, sex hurts and will not be enjoyable.
- It may improve your fertility: This is a no brainer if you want to have babies. The more sex you have, the higher the chance to fall pregnant.

- It relieves menstrual and premenstrual cramps: Some of the neurotransmitters released during intercourse are pain killers. An example is dopamine. It makes you feel less pain.
- Having sex strengthens your pelvic floor. This can help reduce pain during sex and reduce the chance of a vaginal prolapse.
- Reduces vaginal atrophy: Women who continue to be sexually active after menopause are less likely to have significant vaginal atrophy, or the thinning of vaginal walls which can cause pain during sex and urinary symptoms.

## WOMEN DESERVE GOOD SEX

In many cultures, sex is seen as a reward for husbands. Women do not initiate it nor take active part in the process. They do not even speak out or show if they are enjoying it or not. But scientists have revealed that sex is extremely beneficial to women. **Women should therefore not just desire sex, they should initiate it and they should enforce it.**

Wives must understand that it is their right to have great sex with their spouses. This is because sex offers great benefits to their bodies and wellbeing.

### Portia and Phil

*Portia said, "Lack of intimacy is not only a concern for me, it is a real worry that gives me headache. When Phil and I are at each other regularly, not only does it give me pleasure and acceptance; I feel confident and I have so much energy too. When he is not touching me, kissing or caressing me, I have migraines. I am thinking and asking myself, am I not attractive anymore? Psychologically, it messes me up and I develop colds and flu. I do not function well without sex. I feel it is my immune booster."*

**CHECKPOINT**

Share with your spouse any health benefits you have enjoyed as a result of having sex. This could be one recent experience or on-going experiences.

CHAPTER THREE

# Enjoying a Great Sex Life

*Sex is fellowshipping, worshipping and sharing each other's bodies. It involves every aspect of your being: body, soul and spirit.*

Sex itself is not marriage but marriage is sex. Marriage without sex is not only boring but it is like a human body without oxygen. But we must also understand that great sex does not happen without a great lover. Sex on its own cannot be enjoyable without a great lover. It is the lover that makes sex enjoyable.

Sex is one of the most important reasons people marry. It is no secret that most of us, especially men, got married to have the legal right and societal approval for sex. So, if a man is denied sex by his wife, he feels very frustrated and angry. In the same vein, when a woman wants sex from her husband, and she does not get it, she becomes bitter and anxious, thinking that he might be seeing someone else.

Growing up, I witnessed a bizarre thing among married couples in my community. There were fights and quarrels among ladies. These fights were usually between wives and suspected mistresses of their husbands. The wives would be shouting in the neighbourhood, calling the suspected mistresses 'thieves'. What had they stolen? They had had illegal sex with their husbands! That was the only thing the women fought over. This shows the extent to which both men and women cherish sex in their marriages.

Sex is fellowshipping, worshipping and sharing each other's bodies. It involves every aspect of your being: body, soul and spirit. When couples make time and put in the effort to make it happen, it is the most pleasurable thing ever. Sex is an art, the more we practice, the better we become at it. Women are known to be keener on the romance and foreplay side of sex. It is important to them. They want to be embraced, accepted and feel connected to you. They want to be cuddled and appreciated. Every woman also wants to be pampered, adored and loved with good words that are soothing to the body, soul and spirit. That is what I call sexual worship.

Sex is the glue that binds couples together. Sex is the X factor. If couples want to have a successful marriage, then they cannot take their eyes off sex. If they want to be happy in the marriage, husband and wife must make every genuine effort to add more spice to their sex life. Sex and prayer are the two acts of worship in a marriage. This helps us to be intimate and deeply connected. The more couples have sex, the better they become emotionally and spiritually connected and attached.

Sex brings happiness. Researchers agree that couples who have regular sex are healthier, more glowing and happier than couples who don't. In a marriage where couples have regular good sex, they tend to look happy and healthy. But what I say is that this does not even require research. When couples have good sex, they look at each other's faces with broad smiles. They appreciate each other more. There is a great vibe at home that day. Everybody is in their very best mood. Sex indeed is like spices that increase the aroma of a stew and make it taste better. It is like the Red Bull drink that gives you wings. It is the power for your day. If you deny each other, you are missing out on a lot. Couples should get back to the basics and renew their sex life.

If couples do not learn the art of good sex, it can be boring, repetitive and unattractive. Couples who are bitter, angry, disconnected and unforgiving will struggle to enjoy sex. At best, just one person may selfishly enjoy it but not both.

> *Joe has been married to Cathy for 7 years. Joe says, "Sex kept us very close together in our first 3 years of marriage. It was an amazing time in our marital life. Sex and romance gave us something to look forward to every evening. I enjoyed Cathy and she probably enjoyed me as well. In fact, we were just inseparable. The last 3 years following the birth of our two kids have been very difficult. Even though we sleep on the same bed, I miss Cathy so much."*
>
> *Cathy also had this to say, "It is sad to think that we have come to the end of our sexual journey. We*

*have not spoken a lot about it. And neither one of us wants to initiate it. With no sexual intercourse, we are drifting apart each day."*

**CHECKPOINT**

How do you feel when you go a long time without having sex? Discuss the reasons you are not having regular sex with your partner.

## GREAT SEX DOESN'T JUST HAPPEN

There is good sex and there is great sex. And there are times you just do not feel for it but you have sex anyway because your partner requested it. Sometimes, it is just the fun of it, not much effort is put into it. There are other times too when the woman is ovulating, and all that she wants is that sperm to give her a baby. In that case, she does not care about good or great sex.

Good sex requires the lovers' total commitment to making it happen. Great sex requires quality time, deep affection, smart preparation and good communication. If couples ignore these key ingredients and expect to have good sex, it may not happen.

Many marriages terminate because couples think they are no more attracted to each other sexually. This happens when couples take their sex life for granted. They may have ignored the key ingredients that lead to good sex.

Great sex is a process and action that involves love, quality time, unhindered communication, deep desire, passionate kissing, and fearless licking. It also includes expert touching, genuine worshipping, skilful fondling, welcomed penetration, intense orgasm and undisturbed relaxation.

When two people involved in love affairs are locked with each other's bodies in compromising positions with their skin rubbing on each other, they are accelerated onto cloud nine. Here, there is a release of intense pleasure, joy, heat and ecstasy. When this intense pleasure and joy is sustained over a period of time, couples forget their environment and surrounding. This is because certain neurotransmitters and hormones called love hormones are released which intoxicate the lovers with ecstasy.

Couples then burst into uncontrollable screaming as a result of pleasurable penetration. At this stage, every facet of the body, the soul and the spirit receive special nourishment that brings pure joy, vibrant energy and total re-awakening to their bodies. Both husband and wife let themselves go. Such couples have forgiven and forgotten all hurts. They have accepted each other's naked bodies. They worship each other's bodies with words of adulation, affirmation and affection. Here, both husband and wife want to spoil each other with love, love and more love. Couples also use their tongues, hands and ultimately their sexual organs for effective pleasure and absolute satisfaction. At this level, the couple desires more and more sex. It is a simply magical and unforgettable moment. That is what I call great sex.

This usually follows with irresistible rest, welcome relaxation and deep sleep as the couple are locked in each other's bosom. Such great moments of pleasure are also a function of appropriate time and undisturbed location. Reaching such a crescendo requires the couples' total and undivided attention, confidence in each other and safety in the location.

**CHECKPOINT**

Discuss with your spouse the things that can enhance your intercourse.

## WHY TIMING IS IMPORTANT IN SEXUAL INTERCOURSE

> *"There is a time for everything,*
> *and a season for every activity*
> *under the heavens…"*
>
> ECCLESIASTES 3:1 (NIV)

When it comes to sex, it is often said that men are always ready but women are not. Even though there is some truth in this, it is not always true for every man. I know this from a personal point of view as a man and friends I talk to. Just as a woman needs time for sex and functions better during certain times, so do men.

Women say they need time to prepare themselves before inviting you to their kingdom of many wonders. When a woman feels unclean she does not feel confident. So, when you are heated and she asks for permission to visit the bathroom first, you must grant the request with no questions asked!

The menstrual period is another one. A woman feels horny for about two weeks before her period—that is the ovulation stage. Researchers believe that high libido is due to an increase in oestrogen and testosterone levels. This is also the time the woman is likely to fall pregnant if she has sex, especially 2-3 days to menstruation. Women are therefore wired by nature to desire sex around this time. So men who want women to give them great sex should target this time. But remember she is the most fertile at this time so if you don't want babies, be careful.

Trying to have sex when the kids have not gone to sleep is bad timing for the woman. She needs a clear mind to have great sex. Is the door shut properly? Are the children sleeping? Timing is so important to the woman. It is in their nature to be patient, caring and understanding.

> *Eric 41 complained, "I think my wife intentionally keeps herself so busy, especially after 9 pm. She finds every excuse to be unavailable. When she finally comes to the bedroom at 11 pm and finds that I am still awake, she will enter the bathroom. There, she spends at least one hour. By that time I give up and go to sleep. In the end, I do not see what time she comes to bed. This is not an occasional occurrence, it happens every day. If this is not a deliberate and evil attempt to punish me, then I don't know what else it is. The question is how much time should I give to her?"*

> *During counselling, Esther lamented, "I am left to do all the house chores every evening, even though we both work full time. Joe just goes to bed waiting for me to finish all the house chores and then pounces on me like a cat chasing a mouse. In fact, sometimes I pray for the spirit of sleep to fall on him when I am having my shower. By the time I come to the bedroom, he is snoring and I sneak under the duvet."*

This tells you that when women are very tired in the evening, they have no energy or desire for intercourse. The woman needs to first unwind and relax before sexual intercourse. If men want their women to be available for them, then they should support them at home. Free her to have more time to rest and relax her body. Help her de-stress. Listen to her chatter about work, the kids and so on. Calm her fears and nerves. And the gate of heaven is almost open for free entry.

Men are not always ready either. Men also have their own issues which require that they unwind from certain stressful situations before they have sex.

What about early morning sex? This is a blockbuster time for both genders. Ladies, do you remember when you had to take early morning urine (Emu) for a pregnancy test? Oestrogen levels are highest in females early in the morning. And testosterone levels are also highest for males in the morning. It is the reason men are hard in the morning and women feel cuddly as well. It is one of the best times for sex if you are not working. You can be late to work if you have morning shifts, so you need to plan well.

**CHECKPOINT**

Discuss what times you usually enjoy sex with your partner. List reasons and things that contribute to that.

CHAPTER FOUR

# Enjoying the Art of Foreplay

*Prayer and Bible study are great*
*but they will not give you great sex.*
*It is not God's duty to make your sex life attractive.*
*It is your responsibility.*

You have to be sensual and creative if you want to have great sex.

Good and attractive sex starts from good foreplay. Good foreplay between the couple is the greatest key to great sex. In fact, most people believe that sex without foreplay is not sex.

If you want to be sexy and romantic, consider the words sensual and erotic.

Erotic is about your sexual desire and pleasure. Sensuality is the ability to fully enjoy your senses. Do you still remember your five senses? Let's refresh our memories. They are: sight, smell, hearing, taste and feel.

## SIGHT—WHEN I LIKE WHAT I SEE

> GENESIS 3:6 (NIV)
>
> *"When the woman saw that the fruit of the tree was good for food and pleasing to the eye, and also desirable for gaining wisdom, she took some and ate it. She also gave some to her husband, who was with her, and he ate it."*

It has been long established that what the eyes see stimulates our appetite, desire and arousal. This is why the internet, magazines, television and books are filled with many sensual images and videos to stimulate our sexual appetite. It is generally accepted that men are the main targets when certain ladies dress provocatively. When you like what you see, it has the potential to turn you on.

Your personality, appearance, and what you wear can be a turn-on or turn-off. It is important to keep our eyes on our shapes and skin. Sex is nothing without the body. Some men are enchanted by a great-looking curvy body. Similarly, some women also find a great physique or a six-pack figure a turn on.

In fact, men respond faster to sexual advances when their wives or partners wear seductive and revealing dresses. Psychologists believe that when the eyes see the same thing over and over, boredom sets in. Wearing new things is a great way to be attractive to your partner. This can be shirts, dresses, underwear, makeup, shoes, and so on. Couples have a duty to arouse each other by wearing things that appeal to the sight of their spouses and by maintaining a good figure.

## SMELL—WEARING SWEET PERFUME DOES A LOT OF GOOD

> SONGS OF SOLOMON 1:3 (NIV)
> *"Pleasing is the fragrance of your perfumes;*
> *your name is like perfume poured out."*

How you smell can turn your partner on or off. Your natural body odour may be what attracted you to your spouse. Historically, certain smells have been considered aphrodisiacs, a subject of much folklore and pseudoscience. Anatomy bears out the link between smells and sex. It reveals that the area of the brain through which we experience smells, the olfactory lobe, is part of the limbic system, the emotional brain, the area through which sexual thoughts and desires are derived (Hirsch & Gruss, 1999).

Researchers found that 25% of patients who suffered a loss of smell also had sexual dysfunction. This is quite scary especially with Covid-19 infecting millions of people and causing them to lose their sense of smell and taste.

Scientists believe that women in particular are so sensitive to smell. They usually like to go out with men whose smell they like. Most men are turned on by the scent of the perfume that women wear. When your partner smells great, it gets you in the mood. When your bedroom smells nice, not only does that get you in the mood for sex, it also enhances sleep.

Both men and women can be enchanted by the perfume that their partners wear. Even at the workplace, I hear women comment positively about the perfume I wear. You can spend some money to buy different sets of perfumes and vary them from time to time.

Going to bed with good perfume is a turn-on for lovers. This also means that good personal hygiene is essential for good foreplay. After you have eaten that spicy food, get rid of that smell before foreplay. It is also imperative to freshen up after cooking, working, walking and sweating to give your spouse good foreplay. Couples who are naked to each other can gently prompt their partners to wash their mouths if their breath is not pleasant. You should not be surprised or angered by such promptings. Couples have a duty to make their spouses want to smell good.

### HEARING—WHISPER A NICE ROMANTIC WORD INTO MY EARS

Hearing is a powerful tool for both pre-and post-intercourse. You feel confident, accepted and loved if your spouse pays you a compliment. The ears of ladies they say, respond quicker to kind words. Intimacy is greatly quickened with words of affirmation and affection. You can enter her palace with thanksgiving and her court with praise. Thanksgiving and praise are not only important to God, females also just don't like it; in fact, they love it. To start any romance with her, she needs your affirmation and acceptance. It is hugely important to her.

Husbands also want to be appreciated for the work they do for the family. Wives should not ignore their husbands. Statements such as "You mean so much to me and the kids for your hard work" get every man to do more. It draws them closer to their wives.

Couples who are open and honest gladly give and accept praise! Good vibes are a turn-on for both men and women but more so for women.

> *Sandy said of her husband Jon, "He makes me feel like a cherished woman. His words are soothing and turn me on. He has a cunning way of licking my neck and touching me softly with his oiled palms. Jon is not rich but he's a great lover. I'm stuck with him forever."*

## TASTE—LET ME KISS YOU

> SONGS OF SOLOMON 1:2 (NIV)
> *"Let him kiss me with the kisses of his mouth—*
> *for your love is more delightful than wine."*

Obviously, your sense of taste comes from your tongue. What you eat and drink will be tasteless without your tongue.

What we taste or eat has a great effect on our sexual desire. Fruits and vegetables are quite good for enhancing our arousal. Dark chocolates are known to boost moods. Herbs and spices such as ginger, garlic, and pepper are all great for sexual boosting.

The tongue is also a powerful organ during foreplay. Licking the appropriate places of the body is a great turn-on for many people. King Solomon understood the power of the tongue. His lover was overwhelmed with how great this king was at kissing. Great kissers always turn their lovers on. In fact, they are very skilled in using their tongues and mouths to arouse and pleasure each other.

> *Abi, a pharmacist in London says, "Sex is like having a meal on your partner. If Phil does not kiss me passionately and from my belly, I do not forgive him. At least he must kiss me and kiss me well."*

Couples must taste and see that their spouses are sweet. It is worth being adventurous at any age. Kissing is great and has many medical or health benefits. But kissers must practise the art and be good at it. Ladies have complained that they get turned off if their partners are bad kissers. Naked couples should talk about this and agree to meet each other's expectations.

### TOUCH – MELT ME WITH YOUR TOUCH

Your hands are a powerful sexual instrument if used skilfully.

Touching each other fondly creates not just heat or warmth, but there is also the arousal of an intense feeling to have sex.

Couples who touch each other more often are connected and engaged. The simple act of hugging, tickling and massaging each other is known to increase affection and release happy hormones such as oxytocin which in turn increase our desire for each other.

The skin is such a powerful sexual organ which gets aroused when it is rubbed or touched. In fact, every part of our skin has receptors to touch known as erogenous zones. Erogenous zones are areas of the body which make us able to feel sexual pleasure. But certain parts of the body have more erogenous zones than others. They make us respond faster to sexual arousal. Everyone is different in responding to touch. It is important to ask your partner if you still don't know. Please don't assume!

> *Prince and Abi have been married for three years in New York. Abi complained, "Prince does not touch me well."*
>
> *Prince confirmed that his former girlfriend loved to be touched on the bum and inside the thigh. Prince assumed that all women preferred to be touched the same way. He was wrong. Abi said, "He has never asked me. I get sexually aroused when I'm touched on my breast but not my nipple."*
>
> *Prince was shocked to learn this. In fact, he thought he was such a great lover touching Abi on the bum and inside her thigh. He had discovered that was not helpful at all but he was prepared to discuss and work on it.*

It is not just the women who want to be touched in a certain way. The men also want their lovers to touch them well. Some men prefer to be touched on any part of their body. They are aroused so long as they find their partners attractive. But most men prefer their spouses to play with their penises. Others prefer their spouses playing with their nipples. Generally, the rule of thumb is, ask!

Men should understand that women do not enjoy you being rough on their skin. They are by nature soft and tender. This is one way they are different from men. They prefer to be rubbed and touched gently. The erogenous zones of women are just right underneath the skin. Men, on the other hand, because of the power of testosterone, have a deep, thick and firm skin. That means that their erogenous zones are deeper under the skin. That is why men also prefer to be touched more firmly.

Couples need to talk about their hot points and how they prefer to be touched. You should not feel shy to guide the hand of your partner where you want to be touched. When your partner gracefully holds or directs your hand, be pleased to obediently follow their lead. This is the beauty of foreplay and lovemaking.

**CHECKPOINT**

Tell your spouse which part of your body you want them to touch during foreplay. Ask them where they want you to touch as well.

CHAPTER FIVE

# Simple Ways to Rekindle Couple's Sex Life

Couples who are quarrelling find it difficult to be naked with each other. Intercourse suffers greatly if couples do not take steps to repair their bridges, appreciate each other, support each other, and make time for each other.

## REPAIR THE BROKEN BRIDGES

For great sex and romance to happen, there is a need for honesty, forgiveness and empathy among couples. Where there is bitterness or unresolved issues, it is difficult to have an intimate relationship. It is important to say sorry the right way. It is also important to forgive your partner and let any hard feelings go. Then you can have a very good fellowship. Don't jump into another lane because there are obstacles in your relationship. Remember that you are part of the solution to every problem in your marriage. Help to build any broken bridges to facilitate easy accessibility. Release each other from emotional pressure and anger. Sometimes, you need to swallow your pride and build up your marriage.

> *Sara and Ed had been on each other's nerves for about two weeks. Sara said, "I was so relieved when Ed finally drew me to himself last night and asked that we have a chat. I was nervous at first but he made me feel like he was the one to blame for all the misunderstanding. He calmed my nerves, looked into my eyes, apologised and comforted me. You can imagine how I felt that night. We had the best sex ever!"*

When any of you is hurting, it is selfish to expect them to have intimate and amazing sex with you. When the hurt and wrongs are corrected, sex is no longer a chore: it is perfect and amazing.

## BEAR EACH OTHER'S BURDEN

You are not going to have great intimacy if one of you is so tired by the end of the day. It is important that you do not leave all chores to one person. Helping out to get things done quickly is to your own advantage. Burdens could be emotional, physical or even spiritual. You must be intimate enough to feel what your spouse feels without them telling you. Good couples usually have telepathy so that they know and feel each other's burdens. If your spouse is upset, your words of comfort and encouragement would be a huge relief to them. They will feel loved and can open up to have sex with you.

*Dani says, "We were really hating each other for the last year. In fact, we were miles apart from each other though we lived under the same roof. Paul would not help me at home, even with the kids. Paul also was angry that he alone paid the bills and rent. Emotions were high anytime we tried to talk about these issues. I was disturbed that we could not agree to support each other until one Sunday we listened to a sermon titled 'Lower each other's burden'. We had a heart to heart talk that night, and we have not been the same since. I give all I earn to the family. Paul plays with the kids, baths Junior, puts them to sleep early. We get to bed early, and cuddle each other. We now have sex four to five times a week compared to the boring and ugly once-a-month sex."*

## TIDY UP THE ROOM

Just as ignition sparks when gas is turned on, both men and women are turned on when the bedroom is loaded with arousing explosives such as sweet aromas and beautiful beddings. It helps to add some colour and glamour to the room. When the eyes see a nice bed, the nose smells a nice aroma, and the ears hear soothing words of affection, everyone is turned on! You all become sensual. What else is needed? All that is required is your availability.

*Eric says, "I married my wife and got another person in addition: homemaker, interior decorator, fashion designer. Marta makes our bedroom very inviting and appetising. Anytime I enter our bedroom, it feels like sleeping in a 5-star hotel. Sex feels so good in our bedroom because of how she decorates our bedroom."*

I recommend that both husband and wife take interest and effort to enhance their bedroom if they want to have great sex. Art, decor and tidiness should be a shared responsibility of husband and wife.

## MAKE YOURSELF AVAILABLE

You can lay the most beautiful bed, light the sweetest candle and wear the best nightdress; they will be useless if your lover is unavailable. This goes to husbands and wives who are so busy during the day that they miss almost all important occasions such as wedding anniversaries or children's birthdays. It is difficult to surprise them because you cannot predict what time they will be home. It is important to ensure that he or she will be available. Make sure such spouses make time for you.

Ideally, you should not compete for your spouse's time and attention. But we know from experience that when your wife or husband becomes the boss of a company or organisation, unfortunately, this job hazard becomes your reality. This happens with ministers of the Gospel, leaders of nations, directors of companies, CEOs and many others. If you are one of such people, it is important to manage your time perfectly well to have a good time for your spouse and children. Have time for romance and sex if you want to have a successful marriage.

*Rita whose husband is a Pentecostal pastor complains, "I married Charles as a Christian but he became a pastor 5 years later. My children and*

*I are suffering because the church has taken him away from us. We hardly see him. It is one meeting and conference after another. We have had just one solitary sex in the last two months. Even that, I had to beg him. This is because he says his job demands are 24/7 which means he is always tired. Our sex life is so poor or non-existent."*

## VARY YOUR LOCATION

Sex should not always take place on your bed. Changing locations can greatly improve the quality of sex.

*Jack 40, said, "I discovered how romantic Sandra is only when we eventually had three nights in Paris after ten years of marriage. I saw things I have never seen in her wardrobe before; I received words I have never heard before, and I heard sounds I have never experienced before." Jack made the holiday an annual affair from thence. They arranged for childcare so that they could have three to four nights away. Sandra confirmed that she felt so good and relieved without the kids. "All my inhibitions were gone, and I was able to express my full self in this 3-star hotel in Paris." Her conclusion was that every couple needs a holiday. "A new environment outside your usual bed is a sex booster."*

## MAKE TIME FOR SEX

Good sex does not start and end in 10 minutes. It could start 24 hours before the sexual activity itself to prepare the mind and the place. Arranging for childcare, finishing work early, finishing house chores early, watching your best films and relaxing your bodies prepare you for great sex. No one enjoys sex when we are tired, worried about the kids, feeling anxious and unhappy.

*Leo and Jo say they ensured their grandma would be available to look after their girls one weekend. On that weekend, they booked tickets for 8pm cinema and followed that up with good sleep but woke up at dawn to enjoy one of the best sex ever.*

Alternatively, it helps to put the kids to bed early so that you can have time for yourselves. Have time to shower together and follow it up in the bedroom.

*Jo said, "The first two years of our marriage were the best in our sex life. When the kids arrived, we seemed to have lost interest and desire for one another. The bedsheet, duvet and the room colours are the same old boring stuff. We have not bought new sets for years. I feel I am sleeping with my brother."*

*Emma, wife of Patrick also said, "I thought we no longer had a physical attraction for each other after fifteen years of marriage. But it all changed with our first holidays in Paris. Come and see! Patrick was all over me, all the five nights we spent there. I had a lot of tips from my friend Agnes on how to spice it up. Every dress or lingerie I wore was just brand new. The perfumes I bought were just irresistible. With hotel beddings changed each day, great food and rest, there was going to be only one winner—great sex!*

## CHECKPOINT

Looking around your house and bedroom, what do you think you can change or add to spice up your sex life as a couple?

CHAPTER SIX

# Why Men Need Sex

To a man, sex is the most important thing in the marriage, and he could be ready for it most of the time. Most men are ready for sex anytime, any day and any place. Give a man good sex and he will do anything for you! He will have extra energy and will become very functional and effective after good sex. Men have increased motivation to run errands and accomplish tasks for their wives when they are pleased sexually. Deny them sex and they are moody, unresponsive and sometimes aggressive. If you want them to be calm, loving and affectionate, then you know what you have to do. There are too many reasons given to why men do better when they have sex. But there is no consistency in the reasons given.

Nonetheless, three important reasons stand out:

1. **High Testosterone**: Testosterone is a sex hormone that plays an important role in the body. In men, it's known to regulate sex drive (libido), bone mass,

fat distribution, muscle mass and strength, and the production of red blood cells and sperm. Testosterone in males is produced primarily by the testicles in cells called the Leydig cells. Women also produce a small amount of testosterone in various parts of their bodies, including the ovaries. Men have approximately sixteen times more testosterone than females in their plasma. This is true and this is easily measured. The typical reference range is 10-30 nmol/l for men and 0.2-1.7 nmol/l for women. Men who have normal levels feel strong, powerful and smart. In fact, just the sight of a beautiful lady can cause a rush of blood flow into the penis resulting in an erection. So, you can understand why husbands may have a stronger desire for sex than wives. It is not their fault. You can blame this on nature.

2. **Sex Brain**: Scientists have shown that the part of the brain responsible for sex is bigger in males compared to females. For this reason, men think about sex at least twice more than women. Some articles even quote as high as 13 times. But the result of such research will depend on the age group of males selected, cultural opinions about sex and also, the conditions under which that research took place.

Again, at conception, the male foetus brain is exposed to a completely different hormonal environment. Scientists believe that during prenatal development, testosterone exposure is directly responsible for masculinising the genitals and brain structures. They believe that this exposure leads to an increase in male-typical behaviour. All that researchers are trying to say is that men should not be blamed if they are promiscuous or think too much about sex because nature has made it so. It is also important to appreciate that women also have other hormones that can make them promiscuous. The bottom line is men and women can be fornicators or adulterers without Christ. It is the discipline and self-control that the Spirit of God gives believers that help to stay with one lover.

3. **Anatomical position of the penis**. This is also not hard to tell. It is so close to the body. Men get aroused when they see naked female bodies. Men also play with their balls and penises due to their anatomical position. This means that even if his wife does not play with his penis, he will do it himself. He does not need to go and hide and undress first to have access to it compared to a woman.

## SAMPSON AND JULIE

*Sampson, a headteacher and church board member lives in Ghana with his wife Julie, an accountant. Life has become very difficult with constant quarrelling. Julie is 52 and going through menopause. She finds Sampson's demand for sex and his insatiable desire for sex too irritating. The marriage is now on the brink of divorce.*

*"We both felt we needed to give each other space. So, I took two weeks' annual leave to be with my parents in the village. When I came back, my 17-year old maidservant had also been sent to the village by Sampson on the same day I was returning. Five months later, the girl and her parents came to see us. Guess what had happened? Aisha was pregnant. She swore that my husband was responsible, even though my husband was denying it. I have no doubt he did it."*

When men are burning with sexual passion the last thing you want to do is to leave them alone with any woman other than their own wives. Put aside spirituality and status. It is a big temptation not many men will pass on.

The penis needs regular exercise: Just like any muscle, scientists believe that the penis becomes larger and stronger with regular sex. The adult penis is likely to shrink and become weaker if it is deprived of regular exercise or sex for a long time.

For this reason, men who are deprived of sex for a long time usually resort to porn or nudity or erotic novels and films for self-gratification. They also become erratic and disorganised if they do not have sex.

So, ladies, if you want your husband to be organised, efficient and effective, you know what you have to do! Feed them with sex and more sex.

**CHECKPOINT**

Ask your husband how many times in a day they think about sex. Discuss some reasons why women also want sex.

CHAPTER SEVEN

# Low Sex Drive

*Men are givers. But when it comes to sex, nothing frustrates them more than having a strong desire yet being unable to give 100% satisfaction.*

In life, there will always be bad times as well as good times. There comes a time when husband and wife accept the reality of life. Not every day is a sex day!

**WHY DON'T I FEEL FOR SEX ANYMORE ?**

The desire for sex is based on a complex interaction of many things, including physical and emotional well-being, experiences, beliefs, lifestyle, and current relationships. If you're experiencing a problem in any of these areas, it can affect your desire for sex. Both men and women are affected by these factors but some affect each gender differently. Sex life goes downhill when you have too many things on your mind, and when you have health issues, not forgetting another culprit, Age!

## Age Can Wreak Havoc on Your Sex Drive

When we were little, we all desired to grow older one day. We envied how our parents had all the powers and authority over us. We wanted to grow faster so that we could become independent. Nobody, however, told us about the responsibility that comes with it. Nobody told us about the unprovoked pains in the body and joints that come with it. And nobody also told us about the declining libido that comes with it. Unfortunately, growing older means your desire and appetite for sex get lower and lower. This is frustrating for any couple, especially if there is a big age gap between them. This decline in our sex drive is due to the reduction in our sex hormones as we grow past 30 years.

One time, I called one of my best friends in London who was celebrating his 60th birthday to wish him a happy birthday. He was quiet for a brief moment when I finished. He laughed and said, "My friend, I don't see anything great about old age." He carried on, "Old age destroys too many things." This sounded funny at the time, but upon reflection, I couldn't agree more with him. Indeed, too many things take a nosedive, especially in our bodies. I can hear you say old age is great. Truly, old age should be embraced gracefully, but too many things make us anxious and get us concerned at that age. That includes sex life. Couples need to be open and honest about it. They have to accept that changes are inevitable and that those changes have affected their sex life. This acceptance helps the situation and there is no apportioning of blame, or wanting to look elsewhere to satisfy our sexual cravings.

*Mark said, "I know my wife is 50+ and things are not the same. I understand. What baffles me is that her sleeping position has changed since Covid-19 started, even though she never contracted it. She sleeps with her back to the wall and comes nowhere near me. I am only 53 and I want to have sex but it seems the distance between us is too big."*

Several men have had the same complaints. These are usually couples who do not communicate the changes in their bodies. With Mark's issue above, Covid-19 could be blamed for it. But it is also possible his wife is going through menopause. When life reaches this age, your main sexual hormone, which is oestrogen, drastically reduces resulting in hot flashes, mood swings, weight gain, irritability, vaginal dryness and reduced libido or sex drive. At this stage, the last thing on a woman's mind is sex.

Men will be more appreciated if they show understanding, emotional support, and empathy for their wives.

Men should also understand that they will not always be strong sexually because testosterone levels will be going down.

After the age of 40, the concentration of circulating testosterone falls by 1% yearly. Low testosterone comes with associated effects on your body and sex life.

Normal ageing comes with its own sexual pressures:

- Quantity of sex is reduced
- Slowness in getting aroused

- Reduced sex drive
- Less firm erection in men
- Mood changes

These are normal life changes, and couples should not be overly concerned about this. Changes and ageing are inevitable. We should embrace them and make adjustments to our new desires and lifestyle.

### Elder Kings and Mrs Kings

*Mrs Kings complained, "From last year after I turned 52, my sleeping pattern has drastically reduced. I have night sweats and sometimes feel very hot. In the daytime, I seem to lose my temper easily. I am becoming more forgetful and I don't understand. I feel so dry and have no delight in sex. But my husband gets upset when he demands sex and I am not ready."*

*When Elder Kings was asked if he had any idea why his wife had changed, this was his response, "I am not a mind reader. How will I know what is happening to her? She is just punishing me with sex. I married my wife so that I could have sex any time I needed it. Why she has changed, she alone can explain, not me."*

It is important for husbands to be patient and learn to gently support their wives going through these changes. When you are not gentle and sensitive to her, the sex gate can be shut permanently until further notice! Couples should understand that menopause is not a permanent change; rather, it is temporary.

Although many women still have satisfying sex during menopause and beyond, some experience a lagging libido during this hormonal change. Couples can still have sex but they may have to use lubricants to increase lubrication. Long foreplay is also known to improve the wetness of the woman. But above all, wives should communicate their feelings to their husbands. Not all husbands know the effects of menopause. Please don't be angry. Gently and lovingly educate them.

But age alone does not tell the entire story. Not all women or men are in their 40s or 50s. The following are other factors that affect sex drive:

### LACK OF RESPECT FOR EACH OTHER

When you feel disrespected by your partner, the last thing on your mind is sex. The husband expects his wife to respect who he is and the wife expects the same. No one likes to be disrespected, especially in front of children or in public.

Your wife wants to be so close to you. She needs your undiluted Public Display of your Affection (PDA). If you disrespect her in public, it is a big insult and humiliation to her and rightly so. Men should understand that if you reject your wife in public, she would also reject your advances in the bedroom. In much the same way, the husband needs even more respect. When there is mutual respect in the marriage, sex is really enjoyable. If you constantly disrespect your spouse, do not expect him/her to give you the best entertainment and pleasure in the bedroom.

## LACK OF AFFECTION PUTS A DAMPER ON SEX

Affection for each other greatly enhances our sex life. Affection is not saying 'I love you' because you want to have sex. Affection is finding something positive and nice you admire about your partner and saying it like you mean it, even outside the bedroom. Showing affection is an everyday life activity in the marriage that makes your partner feel special in your heart. Affection includes your support at home, kissing, holding, touching and commending! There is always something beautiful about him/her; there's always something your partner has done right for you, for the kids, your family and even for the church for which you can praise them.

If men need more respect, then one thing women need more than men is affection. Man, you must understand this is so important to your wife! Your wife needs affection just as men need sex. When she is feeling good, it is your win. She will bare it all for you, man! This is not hard and this is not rocket science. Pastor, elder, deacon or brother, please stop praying and show some affection and your problems are over! Your lack of affection is the reason she does not like sex!

## UNKIND WORDS ARE ENEMIES OF ROMANCE

Words are so powerful in a sexual relationship. Unkind and unloving words will put anyone off. "I think your weight puts me off sex." Unkind words like this, especially those attacking her body could put you in sexual prison with hard labour indefinitely. Women are like incubators. They store up words. Therefore, men ought to be careful what heat they blow! A

British proverb says, "If you don't have any good thing to say, say nothing!" I have learnt this the hard way! Your wife feels super confident to open up, and lay bare for you when she hears your genuine kind words! But if you criticise her and attack her, she does not feel confident to sleep with you because she is hurting. Similarly, when you compare your husband to another man, he feels hurt and sex or romance will not be on his mind. On the contrary, kind words are an ally of sex and romance. If you want to have a smashing sex life, avoid using rude and unkind words towards your partner.

## POOR SEX ROUTINES REPEL EVERYONE

The same sex routines without innovation and creativity have put many couples off from having sex. A man with bad manners and uncultured sexual habits is more likely to send his wife to a night shift even if he has not booked for it. A woman who does not show interest in sex will also send her husband out to another woman.

Are you a bad kisser, bad at foreplay, and a poor romancer? Your wife is unlikely to want to open up to you. Are you stuck in your old school romance, with no creativity and pleasant surprises? Are you quick to jump on her and begin your press-ups without regard for her feelings? You are probably burning your bridges to her wonderful kingdom. Very soon, you will be banned from setting foot at the door. If you are also quick to ejaculate, leaving her in limbo all night while you snore, I am afraid, you might have to wait for another year before your new application would be considered! Both husband and wife have a duty to be adventurous, creative and romantic.

## EXHAUSTION AND TIREDNESS ARE ENEMIES TO GOOD SEX

Exhaustion and tiredness at work and home are known to affect couples' sexual activity. If either of the couple is working too hard with multi-shift, then clearly this will have a knock-on effect on your sex life. Both husband and wife need help and rest. Rest helps to boost desire and interest in sex.

Other activities such as pregnancy, breastfeeding, and looking after children drain the woman. If all the house chores are left to her without any support, it is fair that all she needs after everything is to sleep without any further disturbances from the man. Several studies have shown that men who support their wives at home have more sex.

## FINANCIAL PRESSURE SHOULD BE ARRESTED

Studies show that couples who are under financial pressure are less likely to enjoy sex. You don't need to be a millionaire to enjoy sex. Generally, men may cope better with financial pressure than our ladies. Remember, women were created to be a help mate. They do not enjoy shouldering all the burdens in the family, and neither do they like being the head. They prefer to have their supporting roles without all the financial pressures.

Man, if you make her the breadwinner and she has to do all the work, you are like Esau, I am afraid you have sold your sex right. You have to go begging anytime you feel for sex! Husbands should try to lessen the financial pressure on their wives if they want them to relax and be more romantic. Men who are also going through sustained financial pressure will struggle to resuscitate the penis. Couples need to work together to ease the financial pressures in the marriage to increase sex and romance.

## EMOTIONAL DETACHMENT BREAKS COUPLES

Human beings are created social beings. "And God said it was not good for man to live alone...." Genesis 2:18 (niv). When couples for any reason are not connecting, they become emotionally detached. This will affect passion and desire for sex. Scientists and psychologists agree that women need more attachment. When a woman does not feel connected to her husband, she feels lonely and anxious. She is asking herself so many questions if she is still good enough. She is also asking if she has offended you, or if her marriage is under threat.

If this is not repaired, she loses interest in sex. She does not want to be naked in front of you just in case you do not find her attractive anymore. When couples are open with each other, they are likely to be attracted and attached to each other. It is important to settle any differences as soon as possible to prevent the devil from taking advantage of any situation. More so, you can fix this by starting to do things together—cooking, walking, praying and kissing.

## MEDICAL CONDITIONS ARE NOBODY'S FAULT

Any medical condition could affect libido and interest in sex. Many nonsexual diseases such as arthritis, cancer, diabetes, high blood pressure, coronary artery disease and neurological diseases can affect sex drive. High blood pressure and diabetes are notoriously unkind to men's genitals. They can damage a man's vascular system and affect his ability to maintain an erection.

Major surgical procedures such as those around a woman's breasts, abdomen, genitals and reproductive organs can impact hugely on her sex drive. She could lose her sensitivity to touch or sexual functions. Again, certain prescribed drugs such as high blood pressure and antidepressants can lower the sex drive of both husbands and wives. As the couple gets older, they are more likely to be on one or more medications. Any such medications can put a damper on sex drive. If your partner all of a sudden becomes disinterested in sex, have a look and check the medicines he or she is on.

Covid-19 was also implicated in low libido in several marriages. Reasons cited against Covid-19 were that it has either left one of the couples with 'long Covid' which is having symptoms for a long time leaving the spouse with pains and tiredness all the time, or couples keeping a 2-meter distance at home and on the bed, invariably affecting intimacy.

## POOR BODY IMAGE LOWERS SELF-WORTH

How we view ourselves is also influenced by our body physique. People who look great have massive confidence and are keen on being naked in front of anyone. On the contrary, people who are bloated and overweight have less confidence and are less likely to be naked for sex. Many conditions and situations can affect your body without your fault.

Certain surgical procedures may leave scars, or cause you to lose tissues or even organs. Visible damage to the body may create an uncomfortable and unpleasant body image. Changes such as pregnancy could affect a woman's confidence. She requires her husband's assurance and acceptance. She is watching your attention on other women. Your comments about her body, if they are not positive, can lead to the shutting of the doors to sex. It is important that both husbands and wives keep their body weight in check. Eat healthily and spend more time exercising. Exercise is known to increase confidence and libido.

## SEXUAL TRAUMA IS A GREAT INHIBITION TO SEX

Sex can only be enjoyed in a consensual relationship. No one enjoys sex when it is forced on them. Sadly, some young men and women have had bitter experiences in their childhood. They have been raped and maimed, leaving them traumatised. To such people, the mention of sex, even in a marital relationship, still leaves them panicking. Unless they get help through prayer and counselling, they will have difficulties enjoying sex. It is always useful to be open to your spouse and discuss this with them.

## SOME VALUES AND BELIEFS ARE INIMICAL TO SEX

Some people have certain beliefs and values borne out of culture, religion, and fear that has never been spoken about or challenged. They hold on to them without discussing them with anyone.

A woman told me that in her church, when one is fasting, sex is not allowed, whether any of the couple is also fasting or not. Another woman also told me that a husband should never see the nakedness of his wife; otherwise, he will soon get fed up with it and start going for a new one. She believes that a woman's body should be kept secret from the husband. In fact, she does not have sex in the light or daytime. Can you imagine this? One man also believes that women have another three days to purify themselves after menstruation.

That is why it is important to discuss all matters pertaining to sex and marriage.

## UNRESOLVED CONFLICTS ARE A TURN-OFF FOR SEX

Conflicts are one of the dangers to a successful marriage. There is bound to be conflict in every human relationship. It is however the way it is resolved or unresolved that creates the problem. Women are created relational; they value their relationships. In fact, they are unable to fake that all is well if they have problems with you. Another way they are different from men is that if they have grudges which are unresolved, they do not have any appetite or motivation for sex. When you offend her, she expects you to resolve it and if possible, apologise then the heaven gate will be clearly opened without barriers! Men also expect their wives to apologise if they offend them. Depending on your temperaments, this affects some more than others. If you offend a melancholic person and you do not apologise, they will be cold and unreceptive towards you. Don't bother to initiate sex until you have fully resolved the issue.

**CHECKPOINT**

In your marriage, what was the longest period you did not have sex with your partner? List the main factors that you think are affecting your libido. Discuss this with your partner.

CHAPTER EIGHT

# Sexual Infidelity

*Drink water from your own well— share your love only with your wife. Why spill the water of your springs in the streets, having sex with just anyone? You should reserve it for yourselves. Never share it with strangers. Let your wife be a fountain of blessing for you. Rejoice in the wife of your youth. She is a loving deer, a graceful doe. Let her breasts satisfy you always. May you always be captivated by her love. Why be captivated, my son, by an immoral woman, or fondle the breasts of a promiscuous woman?*

PROVERBS 5:15-20 (NLT)

I like the above Bible verses purely because this was considered worthy to be in the Bible and rightly so. If you thought flirting, romance and sex were not spiritual, I hope this will make you think again. After all, you are not more spiritual than the author, are you? This was written by one of the best men in the area of sex and romance, King Solomon. He gave the counsel above because he understood how many men can lust after other women's breasts when they are probably not paying attention to their own wife's.

It is important to understand that it does not matter whichever woman you marry, there is a duty and effort to keep your wife attractive and evergreen. You have a duty to make the marriage work so that you do not lust after anyone.

## DEALING WITH SEXUAL INFIDELITY

Sexual infidelity is where a person in a sexual relationship seeks sexual satisfaction outside his or her relationship. Simply put, cheating or stealing sex when you are still married. In most Christian circles, this is blamed on the devil. But is this always the devil at work? If it is not the fault of the devil, then who and what causes people to have extra-marital affairs?

### Blaming It on the Devil

All bad things can be blamed on Satan. I wish he could change so that he does not carry all our follies. If you blame sexual infidelity on the devil, then one of you or both of you gave him a job to do.

I hear certain head pastors of some churches sleep with the wives of their junior pastors. I have seen apostles of great churches sleeping with other women. Unfortunately, these so called "men of God" blame satan and everybody except themselves.

David was a man after God's own heart. He was not just a King, he was a powerful King. He committed adultery and yet the Bible never accused him of spiritual ineptitude or of being demon-possessed. Listen to how David let his guard down:

2 SAMUEL 11:2-6 (NLT)

*"One evening, David got up from his bed and walked around on the roof of the palace. From the roof he saw a woman bathing. The woman was very beautiful, and David sent someone to find out about her. The man said, "She is Bathsheba, the daughter of Eliam and the wife of Uriah the Hittite." Then David sent messengers to get her. She came to him, and he slept with her. (Now she was purifying herself from her monthly uncleanness.) Then she went back home. The woman conceived and sent word to David, saying, 'I am pregnant'."*

David took responsibility for his weakness when confronted by the man of God.

Let's see what David said:

2 SAMUEL 12:13 (NLT)

*Then David confessed to Nathan,*
*"I have sinned against the Lord."*
*Nathan replied, "Yes, but the Lord*
*has forgiven you, and you won't*
*die for this sin.*

If David did not blame the devil, why can't the New Testament Christians do same?

The devil is not all that powerful but if you drop your guard, he will take advantage and cause havoc. Couples should have barriers in place to protect their sexual desires. You must take responsibility for your Sexual weakness.

> 1 THESSALONIANS 4:3-4 (NLT)
> *God's will is for you to be holy, so stay away from all sexual sin. Then each of you will control his own body and live in holiness and honor— not in lustful passion like the pagans who do not know God and his ways.*

God has expectations. He expects all his children to be holy and righteous. God doesn't trick us; He shows us how to do it. Stay away from sexual immorality and be self-controlled.

A young man once said to me, "Elder, it is not that we don't know about this Bible verse, we actually know it. But it is easier to say it or read it than do it. There are so many problems at home, which make me seek gratification outside my marriage. We have drifted so far apart that we cannot even hold hands, let alone kiss and have sex."

So you see, instead of seeking to resolve every problem at home, the gentleman above thought the easier solution is to have affairs and ignore the wife. If you do not try to solve problems in your marriage but run away from it, you will live to fight it another day anyway. The stakes are too high to start cheating or be unfaithful. You may cheat but remember there are consequences for every action.

## Putting Your Spouse Into a Sexual Coma

It is wrong to deprive your husband or wife of sex without a cause. I know some couples use sex as a punishment if their spouses do not please them. They put them into sexual prison. This is what I term as a "sexual coma".

1 CORINTHIANS 7:2-5 (NLT)

*"But because there is so much sexual immorality, each man should have his own wife, and each woman should have her own husband. The husband should fulfil his wife's sexual needs, and the wife should fulfil her husband's needs. The wife gives authority over her body to her husband, and the husband gives authority over his body to his wife. Do not deprive each other of sexual relations, unless you both agree to refrain from sexual intimacy for a limited time so you can give yourselves more completely to prayer. Afterwards, you should come together again so that Satan won't be able to tempt you because of your lack of self-control."*

The above scripture is very profound, in that God realises that when couples do not have sex for a long time, temptation will be at the corner waiting for them. God the Creator understands what we are made of, and the reasons we may not be able to stand.

Luckily, the scripture did not pick the wife or the husband as the victim. Both husband and wife can be victims of this temptation.

The command is explicit. The husband must satisfy his wife sexually. The wife must also satisfy her husband sexually.

Getting satisfied does not depend on the giver. Satisfaction totally depends on the receiver. We have different levels of appetite, so the wife should not say the husband has had enough. In much the same way, the husband should not say the wife is satisfied!

*In the matters of sex, you must give,*
*keep giving and continue to give until he*
*or she has no room or capacity to receive more.*

Never think for a moment that sex is gross, unholy and ungodly. Sex is great. Sex is godly. God is pleased with couples who take the time to make love to each other. If couples have shame being naked in the presence of their spouses, then there is a real problem in the marriage.

*Don't ever stop dating your wife*
*and don't ever stop flirting*
*with your husband.*

Women can easily slay their husband's sex drive and men can also slay the sex drive of their wives. Be careful you do not slay your spouse's drive and go about seeking sexual intercourse outside your marriage. Unfortunately, when this happens, it can be so subtle that it builds up gradually until the penis and vagina both go into a sexual coma.

Make sex and romance attractive in your marriage so that you do not go out to steal sex from someone who is looking great.

Infidelity in marriage does not just happen. It has many remote and immediate causes.

A friend asked this question, "Is it true that the penis 'dies' if it sees the same vagina all the time."

> *At first, it seemed a silly question so I asked him what he actually meant?*
>
> *He explained that his friend who was 49 years had difficulty making love with his wife Abba who was 45 years old. They had not had sex for 3 months. Neither he nor the wife made any attempt to improve their sex life and none of them complained.*
>
> *Then this friend Jojo realised that his secretary Linda who was 28 years old had a crush on him. He started flirting with her and they went out after work ostensibly for a board meeting in a hotel. All of a sudden, the man had come alive again and his manhood was very excited and doing the work he had not done for a few years. Jojo was in agreement that sleeping with the same woman (his wife) for 20 years was wrong.*

Is Jojo right or wrong? What is the main reason he is feeling strong again with another woman?

### The Verdict

What Jojo is trying to say is that sex with his wife is boring. He is saying that he is not turned on by his wife. He is not finding his wife attractive anymore. In fact, he is finding her more of a sister or a mother than a wife.

How did the couple get here? Are their problems reversible?

Husbands and wives should endeavour to constantly try to engage with their partners sexually. Marriage without sex can be very difficult for the couple. It can drive you away from each other. Psychologists have revealed that when human beings see the same thing all the time, naturally, they crave innovation and newness. If you do the same thing all the time, you lose interest and seek something better elsewhere. This is your marriage. It is your project. You must be creative and innovative. Spend time and money to bring it to life.

Couples who have similar issues as Jojo and Abba can do a few things to help enhance sexual intercourse.

- Firstly, find time to talk about how both of you feel about the lack of or insufficient sex.
- Discuss possible adjustments you can both make. This can include changing location, e.g. going on holiday, or spending a night or two at a friend's house.
- Be healthy and attractive.
- Check your health and fitness.

- Check how each of you presents yourselves. Are you attractive to each other?
- Check if you have been wearing the same things all the time. Can you freshen up with your undies, makeup, etc.
- Date your wife. Let your wife feel special by taking her out for dinner. Take her to the cinema. You can also go out sightseeing.
- Flirt with your husband. Dazzle him with what he wants to see. You are never too old to dress to tease him.
- Feel good with good makeup and dresses that say 'look at me'.
- Buy her little gifts and flowers. Most women love flowers if not all of them. They are not expensive. Don't wait until their birthday or Valentine's day. You can always buy flowers for at least a fiver.
- Pay each other compliments. Spoil each other with words of endearment.
- Keep up with your appearances. It is natural that as you age things will not be the same. But you can always look attractive! It requires effort and determination.
- Change your sex routines. You see, none of you is a missionary or preacher. But if all you know about sex position is 'missionary position', this can be very boring and can put any of you off. There are many ways to add innovation and style to your sexual intercourse. Be adventurous if you want to enjoy each other.
- Don't just jump into sex without doing the needful. Have great foreplay.

*"You say, "I am allowed to do anything"—but not everything is good for you. And even though "I am allowed to do anything," I must not become a slave to anything. You say, "Food was made for the stomach, and the stomach for food." (This is true, though someday God will do away with both of them.) But you can't say that our bodies were made for sexual immorality. They were made for the Lord, and the Lord cares about our bodies."*

1 CORINTHIANS 6:12-13 (NLT)

## OTHER REASONS FOR INFIDELITY

Other reasons for sexual unfaithfulness could be spiritual, physical or emotional, psychological or hormonal.

### Physical

The Bible says angels do not marry because they do not have a physical body. We are privileged to have physical bodies.

MATTHEW 22:30 (NIV)

*"At the resurrection people will neither*
*marry nor be given in marriage;*
*they will be like the angels in heaven."*

Our physical bodies are the first point of call in getting noticed. Both men and women have a duty toward each other to be physically attractive. Present yourself in an irresistible way to your spouse. Let him or her desire you. Let him or her feel proud of you. Let your skin be like a magnet to him or her. This is because both men and women are visual.

It is true that men indeed are attracted to women who are good looking and have a great shape. So are women. Both men and women get attracted to people who are good looking. Women talk a lot about men who are physically attractive and good looking, especially in Europe. At my office which predominantly has women, anytime we are interviewing for any position, it is the boys that the girls gossip about. Anytime a good looking male contractor visits our office, the ladies pass many comments that I am not able to print, even in my presence.

This is the reason women and men in Europe are obsessed with gyms and dieting. These two areas are multi-billion dollar industries. Men want to get noticed and women also want to get noticed apart from the health benefits. They want to be physically attractive. Young ladies are already beautiful and yet they keep pushing to even look more attractive. Wives have a duty to protect their husbands and husbands also have a duty to protect their wives.

We know in the Bible that Adam screamed just at the sight of the shape and curves of Eve, because she was so beautiful.

> **Genesis 2:15 (NIV)**
> *"The man said,*
> *'This is now bone of my bones*
> *and flesh of my flesh;*
> *she shall be called 'woman,'*
> *for she was taken out of man.'"*

Wives, you can also make your husbands scream in admiration! I know some wives are already mesmerising their husbands.

## Physical Exercise is Good For All

1 Timothy 4:8 (NIV)
*"For physical training is of some value,*
*but godliness has value for all things,*
*holding promise for both the present*
*life and the life to come."*

It is very important for couples to work on their physical bodies. If you cannot exercise, you may consider reducing your food intake.

Sadly, most African couples are guilty of this. We are not only killing our libido, we are actually shortening our lives with too much food and no exercise.

There is no point in accusing your wife that she is bloated when you have no desire to exercise yourself. Husbands must acknowledge that they are the leaders in their marriage. You must lead and your wife will follow.

Prioritise your health above all things if you want to live long. If you want to have good sex, you need a good functioning body. If you want your spouse to desire you all the time, then take your body seriously.

Rigorous and anaerobic exercise helps us to cope with chronic pains by activating our bodies' natural painkillers. Endorphins such as serotonin, dopamine, and oxytocin don't only help us to feel good, but they help us to feel less bad.

If you don't want your spouse to envy friends' spouses, then work on your body. Good bum, good shoulders, flat tummy and strong shoulders are always desirable. A good body makes you feel good and confident to flirt with your spouse. But they do not just happen naturally. It requires conscious efforts to have an enviable and attractive body.

### Excuses! Excuses!! Excuses!!!

I can hear you screaming, 'I am a pastor', 'I am a doctor', 'I am a busy person'. My day starts very early and I don't have time. It is true that if you have no one to support you it can be hard to have the motivation.

We all have 24 hours to use in a day. If Boris Johnson runs with the help of a training instructor after he nearly died of Covid-19, then you too can prioritise your time. Boris is the Prime Minister of the UK and he must be extremely busy but on realising he nearly died of Covid-19 because he was overweight, he began to prioritise his health above all things. We know this when he granted an interview to Sky News as he attempted to encourage healthy living. You can find this on the link below:

> https://news.sky.com/story/pm-targets-checkout-sweets-and-buy-one-get-one-free-deals-in-national-obesity-plan-12037000

Discipline, self-motivation and determination are all you need. You don't need a gym.

Walking, running, and YouTube aerobics, all cost absolutely nothing. Make a decision today for the sake of your marriage, children and your own health to start some exercise.

Eating without burning calories has only one outcome, weight gain.

### Emotions

Emotional issues can be subtle but can have a serious effect on couples and their families.

**DAVID AND AMANDA'S CASE STUDY:**

> *Amanda is a 41-year old nurse who lives with her husband David who is 45 years old. The couple has two children, a 12-year old and a 14-year old. Sex has dried out completely in the marriage in the last year. The last time David raised the issue with Amanda was 6 months ago but it did not end well with the couple blaming each other. This has brought tension into the marriage. The couple came for counselling at the behest of Amanda.*

This is what was revealed: Both have resigned to a sexless marriage because they were not good for each other.

Amanda was having an affair with a male colleague at work who made her feel like a woman.

David was also flirting with a lady at work who really fancied him but they had not had any sexual intimacy yet.

## How Did the Couple Get There?

From Amanda…

- David forgot her birthday and did not apologise or make it up to her.
- David buys her no flowers even though she has said she loves flowers.
- David compared the last dress she wore to her old grandma's.
- When David wants sex, he does not prepare Amanda.
- David finishes sex and goes to sleep.
- She also feels too tired at home most of the time.
- The guy at work boosts her energy.

Let's hear from David:

- Amanda does not dress properly and attractively.
- Amanda is not watching her weight which makes him critical of her.
- Difficulty having an erection at home.
- Instant erection when flirting with Emily at work.
- Gets stressed with financial pressures at home.

Both David and Amanda accepted they have contributed to the problem at home. The good news is that none of them played the devil and spirituality card. This made counselling a bit easier. David and Amanda agreed to work together to make their marriage work.

CHECKPOINT

What do you recommend both Amanda and David should do to overcome this current situation they find themselves in?

## AVOID SEXUAL INFIDELITY AT ALL COSTS

One of the most commonly cited causes of infidelity is the loss of emotional connection with your partner. The person committing the infidelity will often describe having felt unappreciated, lonely, and sad. That is the reason why you should make your partner your friend so that you can have good communication and a good laugh.

Sexual infidelity hurts yourself, your partner and the family. It leaves a stain and dent on you. Do well to avoid it at all costs.

### Elder Dan and Deaconess Dana

*Elder Dan 51 is married to Deaconess Dana 48, both Pentecostal church leaders. They have been married for 25 years with 3 teenage children. They have gone through a very expensive divorce recently. Elder Dan is going through depression as a result of this and sought counselling. He said, "If I had to live my life again, I would pay attention to my wife and children.*

*My marriage was not working but because I am a church elder, I brushed it under the carpet so that it did not come to light. I pretended all was well. When my wife suggested we see a counsellor, I refused. I focused all my attention on my job, social and church standing. I became too close with my work colleague and had an affair with her. I got caught by my wife. I have now lost my wife whom I love, my children, my reputation, my eldership, my standing in Christ and all my property that I have worked so hard for. I can't eat, sleep or pray. I am in a mess."*

### Keep Your Marriage Vow

You should respect that vow you said in the presence of many witnesses before God. "In sickness and in health, till death do you part". When you cheat, you are sinning. The marriage bed should be kept pure.

HEBREWS 13:4 (AMP)
*"Marriage is to be held in honour among all [that is, regarded as something of great value], and the marriage bed undefiled [by immorality or by any sexual sin]; for God will judge the sexually immoral and adulterous."*

### It is an Insult to Your Spouse and Loved Ones

Infidelity brings a big shame on your partner and the family. Partners feel they were not good for you. You disrespect them and all those who supported your marriage.

### Hindrance to Your Prayer Life

It is a sin and it blocks your prayer unless you sincerely apologise to your partner and ask his or her forgiveness and confess to God. If you don't want your prayer to be blocked, please do not cheat on your partner. Just as Adam and Eve went hiding, when we fall short of God's command, we want to hide from Him. Prayer becomes difficult because the devil will drum it in your ear until you give up in prayer. The devil is the accuser of brethren. As soon as you stand to pray he will accuse you. Sin, therefore, prevents God from answering our prayer if we ever manage to pray.

> ISAIAH 59:1-2 (NIV)
> *"Surely the arm of the Lord is not too short to save,*
> *nor His ear too dull to hear. But your iniquities*
> *have built barriers between you and your God,*
> *and your sins have hidden His face from you,*
> *so that He does not hear."*

We will do ourselves a great service if we avoid infidelity and any sins because that is the only reason God does not hear prayer.

### Love For God

If you love God, and His Word abides in you, then you should not do this. The Bible says if you love God keep His word. If you profess to love God, then respect the spouse in the name of God and avoid infidelity.

JOHN 14:15 (NKJV)
*Jesus said, "If you love Me, keep My commandments."*

Loving God is not just mere rhetoric; it is an action and a call to duty. In marriage, you prove your call and fulfil your ministry. In fact, your ministry must start from your home. You must first set an example for your children and family.

### Protect Your Hard-Won Reputation

It is a dent on your reputation, especially for your friends and family who trusted you. You have a duty to protect your hard-earned reputation. You may not know but I can tell you that there are more people who trust you, and believe you because you inspire them. You are a model to them. They will be absolutely disappointed to hear you are cheating on your spouse. Elder Dan above tried it and greatly regrets his unfaithfulness. To protect your reputation is not by covering up your sin and infidelity, it is by avoiding it. It is by refusing to yield to sexual temptation and any temptation. This is how you protect your reputation!

### Prove Your Discipline

Everyone including your spouse gets tempted all the time. The reason they have not yielded is their discipline, determination and perseverance. You must do the same. Christians are admonished in the Bible not to fall into temptation. In fact, God always opens a window of escape. It is up to you to open your eyes to find it. But in the matters of sexual sin, the best remedy recommended by the Bible is Fleeing.

> 1 CORINTHIANS 6:18 (NIV)
> *"Flee from sexual immorality. All other sins a person commits are outside the body, but whoever sins sexually, sins against their own body."*

You cannot overcome sexual sin by standing and praying to God to help you. You cannot kneel and pray for help. It is a call to run and run hard for your life. Keep your discipline and protect your marriage.

## The Quickest Way to Divorce

Be aware that infidelity can lead to separation and divorce. Divorce is too expensive a cost—emotionally, mentally and spiritually. The cost to children can never be estimated. It affects their performance at school, exposes them to the risk of truancy and associating with bad friends, rebellion against teachers and parents. It can be devastating. Remember God does not condone divorce. In fact, God actually hates divorce. So do not let your action or your unfaithfulness lead to divorce.

> MALACHI 2:16 (NLT)
> *"For I hate divorce!" says the Lord, the God of Israel. "To divorce your wife is to overwhelm her with cruelty," says the Lord of Heaven's Armies. "So guard your heart; do not be unfaithful to your wife."*

The above text means God does not just hate divorce; in fact, He hates those who make it happen. He is merciful and just but do not do it and go asking for forgiveness.

## Infidelity Can Cost You Heaven

If you are religious or a Christian, I believe your ultimate aim is to go to heaven. Do not trade your heaven for just a one-night-stand or momentary pleasure.

> 1 CORINTHIANS 6:9 (NLT)
> *"Don't you realise that those who do wrong*
> *will not inherit the Kingdom of God?*
> *Don't fool yourselves. Those who indulge*
> *in sexual sin, or who worship idols,*
> *or commit adultery, or are male prostitutes,*
> *or practise homosexuality."*

Heaven is real and you cannot sacrifice anything for it. Missing out on heaven is the most expensive thing ever to happen to you. Do not let marriage send you to hell!

Your marriage must make you a better person. You must make your spouse a better person. Your marriage should prepare you for heaven. Your marriage should help you to go to heaven. Under no circumstance should your marriage prepare you and your spouse for HELL.

CHECKPOINT

Have you ever been tempted to cheat on your partner? If you avoided it, how did you do it? And why did you consider having extra-marital affairs in the first place?

## CONCLUSION

Marriage will be hugely successful and happy if couples communicate their feelings freely without emotions. Sex is an art. The more we practise, the better we become. To have a great sex life requires energy, time and affection. Both husband and wife have a duty and responsibility to ensure great intimacy and sex in the marriage.

# BIBLIOGRAPHY

Taryn Hillin (2014). 1 in 5 people hide secrets from their spouses. https://www.huffingtonpost.co.uk/entry/secrets-survey-_n_5642818. Accessed 1.1.22

Sergeant, M.J.T., Dickins, T.E., Davies, M.N.O. & Griffiths, M.D. (2007). Hedonic ratings by women of body odor in men are related to sexual orientation, Archives of Sexual Behavior, 36, 395-401.

Mark Griffith (2019). The Science of Sex and Smell, A brief overview of olfactophilia. Psychology for today. https://www.psychologytoday.com/gb/blog/in-excess/201910/the-science-sex-and-smell. Accessed 7.5.2022

Virginia Pelley, (2019). What keeping secret does to your marriage. https://www.fatherly.com/love-money/help-be-more-confident-in-bed. Accessed 1.1.22

Nicky and Sila Lee, (2005). The Marriage book. Alpha International Publications. London.

Daphna Joel (2015). No such thing as 'male' and 'female brain'. https://english.tau.ac.il/news/male_female_brain. Accessed. 08.01.2022

Gray J. (1998). Mars and Venus Together Forever. Vermilion London

Paget L. (2002). How to Give Her Absolute Pleasure. Piatus, London.

Ann summers. https://www.dailypost.co.uk/news/uk-world-news/ann-summers-reveals-how-often-17294510. Accessed 9/1/2022

Catherine H, Mercer Kaye, Wellings Anne M Johnson (2013). Sexually Transmitted Infections 2013; 90 80-81

Kaye Wellings, Melissa Palmer, Kayuzo Machiyama, Emma Slaymaker (20190. Changes in, and factors associated with, frequency of sex in Britain: evidence from three National Surveys of Sexual Attitudes and Lifestyles (Natsal) BMJ 2019; 365

Wales online. Fewer than half of Britons having sex at least once a week. https://www.walesonline.co.uk/news/uk-news/fewer-half-britons-having-sex-16239692' Accessed 23.12.21

Ann Summers (2019). Positive pleasure project research. https://www.dailypost.co.uk/news/uk-world-news/ann-summers-reveals-how-often-17294510. Accessed 7.1/2022

Glezeman M. (2016). Yes, there is a female and a male brain: Morphology versus functionality. PNAS, April 5, 2016 | vol. 113 | no. 14 |

Abramov I, Gordon J, Feldman O, Chavarga A (2012). Sex & vision I: spatio-temporal resolution. Biol Sex Differ 3(1):20.

Glezerman M. (2016). Yes, there is a female and a male brain: Morphology versus functionality. Proc Natl Acad Sci USA 113:E1971

Joel D, Fausto-Sterling A. (2016). Beyond sex differences: new approaches for thinking about variation in brain structure and function. Philos Trans R Soc Lond B Biol Sci 371(1688):20150451.

Breedlove, S.M. (1994). Sexual differentiation of the human nervous system. Annu. Rev. Psychol. 45: 389–418

Alan Hirsch & Jason Gruss (1999). Human male sexual response to olfactory stimuli. Journal of Neurological and Orthopaedic Medicine and Surgery, 19, 14-19

Health benefits of having sex. https://www.dailymail.co.uk/health/article-6638587/Regular-good-sex-lower-blood-pressure-successfully-medicine-scientists-claim.html. Accessed 6.9.22

Sleep and sex. https://www.healthline.com/health-news/having-sex-more-often-can-help-you-sleep-better#Does-having-sex-help-you-sleep-better? Accessed 7.9.22

Sex improves immune system. https://www.webmd.com/sex-relationships/guide/sex-and-health#1. Accessed 7/9/2022

Health benefits of sex. https://www.healthline.com/health/healthy-sex-health-benefits. Accessed 6.9.22

Stuart Brody. (2010). The Relative Health Benefits of Different Sexual Activities. J Sex Med 2010; 7:1336–1361 review

Thomasy Hannah (2022). Having more sex can reduce the risk of prostate cancer. https://www.fatherly.com/health-science/more-sex-ejaculation-masturbation-lower-prostate-cancer-risk

# NOTES

Printed in Great Britain
by Amazon

10448719R10171